RULES OF THUMB

BY TOM PARKER

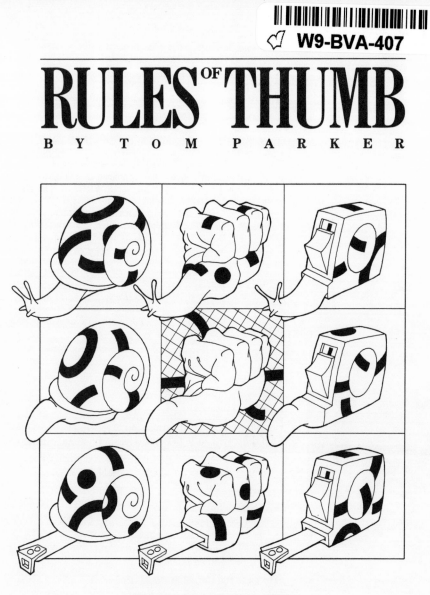

Illustrations by the Author

HOUGHTON MIFFLIN COMPANY BOSTON

Copyright © 1983 by Tom Parker
All rights reserved.

For information about permission to reproduce selections
from this book, write to Permissions, Houghton Mifflin
Company, 2 Park Street, Boston, Massachusetts 02108.

Library of Congress Cataloging in Publication Data

Parker, Tom.

    Rules of thumb.
    Includes index.
    1. Handbooks, vade-mecums, etc. I. Title.
AG106.P37 1983   031′.02   83-17167
ISBN 0-395-34642-8 (pbk.)

Printed in the United States of America

DOH 20 19 18 17 16 15 14 13 12 11

for my mother,
Mary Ellen Parker

A NOTE ABOUT SOURCES

Each rule of thumb is followed by a source, or a rumored source, or the name of the first person to send it in. The people listed are not necessarily claiming a rule of thumb as their own invention. A lot of people sent in rules that they learned from someone else. Many sent clippings or paraphrased another source. Some rules arrived as hearsay. If traveling by word-of-mouth has changed your favorite rule of thumb for the worse, let me know. If, on the other hand, you find it improved, take it as a compliment . . . a good rule of thumb has a life of its own.

THANKS

First of all, thanks to Caroline Eckstrom,
Cheryl Russell, and Richard Eckstrom. They
put up, and put up with, the most.

Thanks to Kat Dalton for her painstaking
work on the shape and design of this book.

Thanks to Michael Rider for his patient help
and advice.

Thanks to *CoEvolution Quarterly*, its staff
and its clever readers.

And a special thanks to all the alert and en-
thusiastic people, many not listed in this edition,
who took the time to mail in rules of thumb.

A RULE OF THUMB is a homemade recipe for making a guess. It is an easy-to-remember guide that falls somewhere between a mathematical formula and a shot in the dark. A farmer, for instance, knows to plant his corn when oak leaves are the size of squirrels' ears. An economics professor knows from sad experience that inviting more than 25 percent of the guests for a university dinner party from the economics department ruins the conversation. Rules of thumb are a kind of tool. They help you appraise a problem or situation. They make it easier to consider the subtleties of the topic at hand; they give you a feel for a subject.

A hundred years ago, people used rules of thumb to make up for a lack of facts. Modern-day rule of thumbing is rooted in an overabundance of facts. The average person, confronted with a computer, volumes of data, and several Ph.D. dissertations often is as perplexed as a pioneer chemist trying to whip up a little gunpowder without a formula. A pilot in a tight spot doesn't ask questions about aeronautical engineering; a pilot in a tight spot asks "now what?" There are times when you don't need to know the best way to do something. These are times for ballpark figures, for knowing what you probably can get away with.

I like getting away with things as much as the next person. What if I knew a lot of rules of thumb? You've seen movies where someone suddenly is dumped on a desert island or thrown back in time. How would you do in a situation like that? Could you impress your ancestors or do any flashy tricks? I think I'd take along a cheat-sheet; a few thousand rules of thumb could come in pretty handy.

So, disguised as the Alpine Planetarium, I sent letters to everyone I could think of, asking for rules of thumb. I mailed letters to businesses and college newspapers. I made a list of magazines and wrote to everyone on the staff, from the mail clerk to the publisher, hoping to generate office talk and some rules of thumb. A friend quietly entered a rule of thumb notice on a nationwide defense and research computer network.

Old folks responded with the most enthusiasm; good friends, the least. Experts and editors fell somewhere in between. There were people who took days to come up with "The rain in Spain falls mainly on the plain." Others spouted four or five winners off the top of their heads. More than anything, the response was unpredictable. A local guitar maker's favorite rule of thumb had to do with stream morphology. A wind power expert from Cornell sent one on digging graves.

The first batch of rules was published in *CoEvolution Quarterly* magazine with a call for further entries. *CoEvolution* readers sent postcards and letters from as far away as Alaska, Japan, and Australia. I got rules of thumb written on fancy letterheads, computer paper, napkins, stolen office stationery, and airline barf bags. Many people included their ideas about the phrase "rules of thumb." Some suggested that "rule of thumb" refers to the relationship between the human thumb and the length of one inch. Others thought the term came from an old English law that said a man could legally beat his wife and children with a stick no thicker than his thumb.

Frankly, I'm still not sure where the term comes from. I do know that a rule of thumb is not a joke or a ditty. It is not a Murphy's Law. Murphy says that things will take longer than we think: a rule of thumb says how much longer. Neither do most old-time sayings and expressions qualify as rules of thumb: While a proverb says that a stitch in time saves nine, a rule of thumb says to allow one inch of yarn for every stitch on a knitting needle. A maxim cautions us not to risk more than we can afford to lose; a rule of thumb warns us not to lose more than twenty times the betting limit in a single poker game. Most of all, a rule of thumb is not always right. It is simply a personal tool for making things work most of the time, under most conditions.

This book contains what I would call rules of thumb. Some have debatable qualifications. Others have dubious practical value. Most were picked from the Alpine Planetarium mailbag. I've tossed out the duplicates, the grandmotherly advice, and the jokes (at least the bad ones). I'm keeping the good stuff in a cumulative file, stored in a computer — a rule of thumb archive.

When Joe Kaiser of Covington, Kentucky, wants to blow a stump out of the ground, he uses a rule of thumb — one stick of dynamite for every 4 inches of stump diameter. But you don't need a troublesome stump to wonder how much dynamite it takes to blow one up. It's a matter of curiosity. What would it be like to land a Lear jet? How can you tell when someone is stuttering in Japanese? How many people does it take to eat an ostrich egg? This is a book for curious people. It is not a book of facts; it is a book of experience. It is a collection of observations by people who bother to look at how they get things done. It is by people who like to guess with precision. *Rules of Thumb* is dedicated to them.

You are invited to add to our file.

This book is just a start.
Imagine a book with ten or even
twenty thousand rules of thumb.
If you have a rule of thumb
you would like to add to this
collection, mail it to:

RULES OF THUMB

c/o Houghton Mifflin Co.
Two Park Street
Boston, Massachusetts 02108

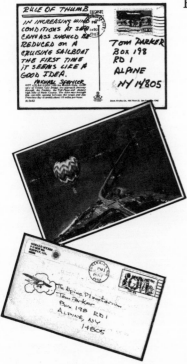

RULES OF THUMB

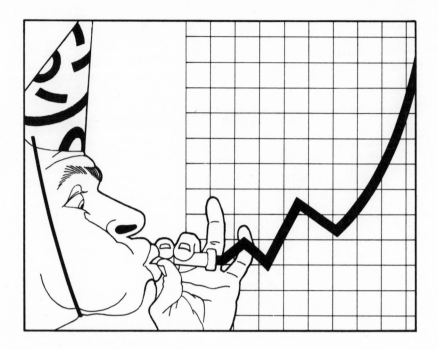

1. PARTY GUESTS   The number of guests at a child's birthday party should be limited to the age of the child. Invite three for a three-year-old, five for a five-year-old.   *Diane Gerhart, accountant*

2. CHECKING DRIED VEGETABLES   Properly dried peas and corn should shatter when hit with a hammer.   *Betsy Cook, Buckinghamshire, England*

3. BLASTING A STUMP   You can blow most tree stumps out of the ground if you use one stick of dynamite for every 4 inches of stump diameter. Trees with taproots take less.   *Joe Kaiser, Covington, Kentucky*

4. EATING POTATOES   People will eat one and a half to two times the number of potatoes mashed that they would eat baked.   *Ned Bounds, sawyer, Salmon, Idaho*

5. TRAINING FALCONS   To find the trained flying weight of a wild caught falcon, subtract 10 percent from the bird's weight at capture.
Douglass A. Pineo, biologist and falconer, Pullman, Washington

6. POLITICAL PLANNING   People moving into a new tract development are politically inert for five years.   *Gary Evans, city planner*

7. SMOKING CIGARETTES   You need three books of matches for every two packs of cigarettes you smoke. *Bob Horton, statistics consultant, West Lafayette, Indiana*

8. SENDING CHILDREN TO SCHOOL   When universal education was introduced in the Philippine Islands there were no birth records and sorting children by age was a problem. The teachers found that a child is old enough to send to school when he can cross his arms over his head and grasp his ears with his opposite hands.   *Anna L. Curtis, Cedar Falls, Iowa*

9. REPOTTING AFRICAN VIOLETS   African violets need small pots. As a rule, the pot should be one-third the width of the plant. A 6-inch plant, for instance, needs a 2-inch pot.
Mary Ellen Parker, teacher, Cincinnati, Ohio

10. DESIGNING A MUSEUM A museum should have office, work, and storage space equal to its exhibit space. *Dr. Gertrude Ward, Richmond, Indiana*

11. ESTIMATING YOUR SALARY To estimate a yearly salary from an hourly wage, double the wage and change the decimal point to a comma. Thus, $3 per hour becomes $6,000 per year. This figure is about 4 percent low, but with taxes the way they are, it doesn't make much difference. *Don Tichnor, farmer*

12. EDITING A MAGAZINE You should plan on reading through at least two hundred unsolicited manuscripts to find one that is usable.
M. Lafavore, editor, Organic Gardening magazine

13. EDITING AN ARTICLE When editing an article, you rarely go wrong crossing out the first page and a half.
Bryant Robey, editor, American Demographics magazine

14. EDITING A MAGAZINE Three double-spaced typewritten pages of manuscript can be edited into one magazine column without anyone, not even the author, noticing that 20 percent of the words are gone. *John Kelsey, editor, Fine Woodworking magazine*

15. AVOIDING A CRASH IN A CAR RACE At high speed nothing stays in the same place for long. Aim your car at the spot where you see an accident start. Chances are the accident will have moved by the time you get there. *Joie Chitwood, former Indy driver and owner of the Joie Chitwood Thrill Show*

16. CURING LUMBER Air-dry lumber for one year per inch of thickness.
John Kelsey, editor, Fine Woodworking magazine

17. ANNOUNCING THE NEWS It takes about one minute to read fifteen double-spaced typewritten lines on the air, or about four seconds per line.
Charles Osgood, CBS news commentator

18. EATING CHEESE   The quality of the flavor of cheese is inversely proportional to the thickness of the slice.   *Jas. C. O'Neill, Baraboo, Wisconsin*

19. ADJUSTING AN ANVIL   Adjust the height of your anvil to match the bottom of your natural hammer stroke.   *Dennis Williams, blacksmith*

20. ADJUSTING AN ANVIL   Stand with your arms at your side. The height of your anvil should be the height of your knuckles.
Charles McRaven, blacksmith

21. ADJUSTING A WORKBENCH   If you stand at attention, your wrist is at the right height for a woodworking bench and your elbow is at the right height for the top of a metal-working vice.
W. Oakley, shop expert

22. LANDING A LEAR JET   A Lear jet 25G will float about 100 extra feet down the runway for each knot over its proper landing speed.
Richard Collins, pilot and writer

23. PLANNING A DINNER   Inviting more than 25 percent of the guests for a university dinner party from the economics department ruins the conversation.   *Martha Farnsworth Riche, editor*

24. SOARING   When flying a sailplane on a cross-country flight, expect thermals to be five times as far apart as they are high.
John Campbell, glider pilot, Ann Arbor, Michigan

25. CHOOSING A BICYCLE FRAME   The crossbar on your bicycle frame should come just to your crotch when you straddle the bike with your shoes off and your feet flat on the ground.
Leslie Warren, music teacher, Kittery Point, Maine

26. CATCHING CRABS IN TEXAS   Crabbing season in Texas consists of all the months with the letter *r* in them. You can catch crabs during the other months but they aren't good to eat.
David Hechler, writer, Rockport, Texas

27. TAKING TONSILS OUT A conservative doctor will recommend a tonsillectomy if a child has seven attacks of tonsillitis within a year, or five in each of the preceding two years. A less conservative doctor will recommend the operation if a child has three to five attacks in each of two consecutive years.
William A. Nolen, M.D.

28. BUYING SOCKS THAT FIT Wrap the bottom part of a sock around your fist. If the sock is the right size, the heel will just meet the toe.
Nelson Smith, physical education teacher, Cincinnati, Ohio

29. LOSING SOCKS You should expect to lose one sock every time you do your laundry.
Robbie Aceto, musician

30. AVOIDING AVALANCHES   A snowfall of 1 inch or more per hour indicates a very high avalanche potential.   *Scott M. Kruse, Yosemite National Park, California*

31. PROFESSIONAL TOOLS   Engineers and computer programmers need equipment equal to one year's earnings to work at top speed. Anything less slows them down.
William Blake, engineering manager, New Haven, Connecticut

32. SELLING THINGS BY MAIL   Most people selling things by mail need at least a 200-percent markup to make money. You shouldn't pay more than $10 for something you sell for $30.
Jim Kobs, Kobs and Brady Advertising, Chicago, Illinois

33. USING SCREWS   To avoid splits when using lag screws in soft wood, drill a pilot hole that is one-half the diameter of the screw thread.
Joseph Smith, carpenter

34. MAIL-ORDER ADVERTISING   Ten to fifteen percent of the people who accept a trial offer will decide for one reason or another to return the merchandise. But, a trial offer will normally produce about twice as many orders as a money-back guarantee.
Jim Kobs, Kobs and Brady Advertising, Chicago, Illinois

35. CHOOSING A BOOT   Generally, the fewer seams a boot has, the better it is. The best boots have only one seam running up the back.
Alwyn T. Perrin, Explorers Ltd. Source Book

36. ESTIMATING THE TEMPERATURE   To estimate the temperature outdoors in degrees Fahrenheit, count the number of times a lone cricket chirps in fifteen seconds and add thirty-seven.
Steven Harper, Big Sur, California

37. ESTIMATING THE TEMPERATURE   When spit freezes before it hits the ground, it's at least 40 degrees Fahrenheit below zero.
Jeanie MacDonough, social scientist

38. SHIVERING Shivering produces as much heat as running at a slow pace or roughly the amount of heat generated from eating two medium-sized chocolate bars per hour.

Peggy Kerber, editor, Mountaineering

39. TRAVELING WITH KIDS Letting your kids chew gum on a trip helps keep them quiet. Kids too small to chew gum will usually sleep.

Gay Dalby Maher, flight instructor

40. LANDING AN AIRPLANE If you haven't touched down in the first third of the runway, abandon the landing and go around for another approach.

Dan Sutliff, flight instructor

41. TAKING OFF IN AN AIRPLANE If you haven't left the ground in the first half of the runway, abort the takeoff. *John Stickle, flight instructor*

42. THE WORK RULE OF TWO Half the amount of work yields twice the results when it occurs outside the market economy.

Dr. Larry R. Hunt, Toronto, Ontario

43. EXPLORING A CAVE You should have at least four people for any caving expedition. If someone is injured, two people can go for help while one stays with the injured caver. That way, no one is in the cave alone. *David R. McClurg, speleologist*

44. SUPERINSULATED HOUSES A superinsulated house should have 12 square feet of windows for every 100 square feet of floor. At least two thirds of the windows should be facing south.

Phillip Close, builder

45. BUILDING A HOUSE An odd-angled wall will cost twice as much as a wall built with 90-degree corners. *Rick Eckstrom, builder*

46. JUDGING THE AGE OF A CALF A calf whose tail nearly reaches the ground is more than a year old. *Edward Dalrymple, dairy farmer*

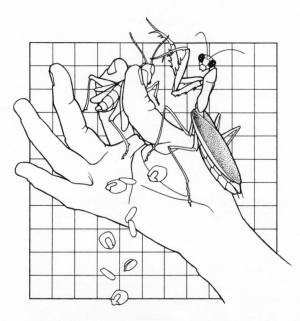

47. PRAYING MANTISES   It takes sixteen praying mantis egg cases per acre to keep other insects under control.   *Ronald Newberry, gardener*

48. BUILDING A MODEL   Experienced modelers routinely scavenge parts from old or unused models or combine one model kit with another. Don't try to match up model kits with more than a 20-percent difference in scale unless you're prepared to do a lot of modification.   *Brick Price, model builder*

49. SHEARING A SHEEP   You can plan on making one sweater for every two pounds of wool you shear from a sheep.   *Mary Catherine, preschool teacher*

50. NURSING HOMES   Patients who are terminally ill are more likely to die after a holiday than before.
Jim Schlobohm, Oak Park, Illinois

51. SELLING THINGS DOOR TO DOOR   After knocking, stand at least four feet back from the door.
Benjamin Snyder, bible salesman

52. BREEDING YOUR COWS   You need one bull for every twenty-five cows.   *Julian Silver, farm hand*

53. TALKING TO FOREIGNERS When you are conversing in your native language with people who don't speak it fluently, assume that they understand about half as much as they look like they understand. *Stephen Cudhea, English-language instructor, Ishikawa, Japan*

54. TALKING TO HIGH SCHOOL STUDENTS When giving instructions to a high school class, you can bet that three students will follow them incorrectly. *David T. Russell, high school teacher*

55. GROWING A TOWEL A 20-by-30-foot patch of ground, sown with two pounds of flax seed, should provide enough fiber to weave a small tablecloth or towel. *Jean Heavrin, weaver*

56. SAILING INTO PORT If the wind is strong, the tide can be wrong; if the wind is light, the tide must be right. *Gary Closter, sailor with a broken engine*

57. DECIDING WHEN TO BLUFF There are three factors involved in successful bluffing. (1.) Your opponent: It is easier to bluff a strong player than a weak one. (2.) Your position in the game: It is easier to bluff a big loser than a big winner. (3.) Money: The bigger the stakes, the easier it is to bluff. Don't bluff unless you have at least two of these factors on your side. *Edwin Silberstang, games expert*

58. DECIDING WHEN TO BLUFF One or two bluffs per poker game are enough. Overindulgence can produce a bluffaholic. *Dale Armstrong, card player*

59. HOUSING PIGEONS The inside of a pigeon loft should be low enough so that a pigeon can't fly over your head and small enough so that you can touch all four walls while standing in the middle. *Dr. Herbert R. Axelrod, retired pigeon racer*

60. BUILDING A DOG KENNEL A kennel should be two times the length of the dog you are building it for. Measure the dog from its nose to the tip of its tail. *Charles Stoehr, dog trainer, Cincinnati, Ohio*

61. MANUFACTURING The materials for a mass-produced electronic device should cost about 10 percent of the retail price of the finished product.
Ray Bruman, Berkeley, California

62. MAKING APPLE CIDER A bushel of apples will make slightly more than three gallons of cider.
Martin Stillwell, farmer

63. MAKING APPLE CIDER It takes three apples to make a glass of apple cider.
States Cider Mill, Odessa, New York

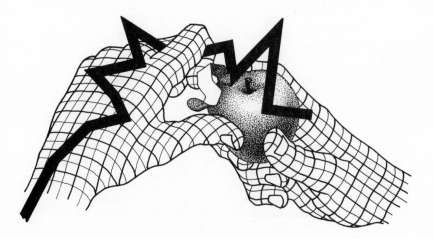

64. CHECKING A FLY ROD A fly rod with reel should physically balance somewhere within 6 inches of the handle.
Sheridan Anderson, author, The Curtis Creek Manifesto

65. DRINKING PROBLEMS The farther north you go, the more drinking is a problem.
Harry Reasoner, CBS News report on alcohol use in Greenland

66. PLANNING A HOSPITAL A hospital should have four to four and a half beds for every thousand people in the community it serves.
Douglass A. Pineo, biologist and falconer, Pullman, Washington

67. TAKING A NEW JOB   When taking a new job, beware of those who are too friendly too soon.
Joel R. Stegall, dean, Ithaca College School of Music, Ithaca, New York

68. BUYING FURS   As a rule, short-haired furs like Persian lamb and mink look best on short people; long-haired furs like skunk and fox look best on tall people.   *Frank G. Ashbrook, biologist and fur-trade expert*

69. FEEDING A BASS   A largemouth bass can eat a fish one-half its length.
Walter Booth, outboard engine repairman

70. BUYING AN INFLATABLE RAFT   As a rule, inflatable boats under 10 feet long are cheaply built.
Alwyn T. Perrin, Explorers Ltd. Source Book

71. TRAVELING IN EUROPE   Count each kilometer as a mile when planning a trip by car. It will take as long to drive three hundred kilometers in Europe as it takes to drive three hundred miles in the United States.   *Robert Cumberford, Austin, Texas*

72. CRACKING A SECRET CODE   If the high-frequency letters *ETOANIRSH* occur very often, in this order, you can assume that you are dealing with a transposition cipher in which the letters remain the same but are rearranged in a new pattern. On the other hand, the repeated appearance of low-frequency letters indicates that a message has been written in a substitution code.
John Laffin, cryptologist

73. POLITICAL CAMPAIGNS   If you are personally canvassing door-to-door within two weeks of an election and three of ten voters both recognize you and give you positive feedback, you will probably win.
Tom Wilbur, county commissioner, East Lansing, Michigan

74. POLITICAL CAMPAIGNS   If more than 40 percent of the likely voters have a favorable impression of an incumbent six months before an election, then he or she is probably unbeatable.
Tom Wilbur, county commissioner, East Lansing, Michigan

75. CAMPAIGNING IN TEXAS There isn't a horse that can't be rode and there isn't a rider that can't be throwed.
John Connally, former governor of Texas

76. LANDSLIDES A bank is subject to landslides and rockslides until enough mud or rock has fallen against it to form a pile of debris, or talus, with a 37-degree slope.
Rob Weinberg, Tassajara Zen Mountain Center, Carmel Valley, California

77. REPRESENTING AN AUTHOR A prospective client for a literary agency who begins his letter of application with the words "My name is . . ." should not be seriously considered. *Walter Pitkin, literary agent*

78. STREAM FISHING FOR TROUT Trout do most of their surface feeding in the upstream third of a pool. *Sheridan Anderson, author, The Curtis Creek Manifesto*

79. SELLING THINGS BY MAIL Past customers will respond three to six times as well as good prospects who are not past customers.
Jim Kobs, Kobs and Brady Advertising, Chicago, Illinois

80. TREE ROOTS You can assume that the roots of normally shaped trees extend at least to the drip line of the branches.
Shelly Wade, tree specialist

81. TREE ROOTS The diameter of a tree trunk in inches is the radius of the root system in feet.
J. T. Schaefer, pilot

82. SINKING EYEBALLS Sunken eyeballs in a sick infant indicate at least 10-percent dehydration. So does a sunken soft spot, or fontanelle, on the top of the head.
James Macmillan, M.D.

83. MAILING A LETTER You can mail five sheets of paper with a 20 cent stamp.
Ron Bean, mechanics of materials student, Madison, Wisconsin

Postcard — address side (Japanese airmail)

郵便はがき

□□□-□□

Tom Parker
Box 198, RD1
Alpine, NY
14805
USA

PARAVION
航空郵便

兼六園と徽軫燈籠

Teramachi 2-12-6, Kanazawa,
Ishikawa-ken 921 JAPAN

金沢南郵便局

Postcard — Stephen Cuellca

Dear Mr. Parker,
When you are conversing in your native language
with people who don't speak it fluently, I assume
that they understand about half as much as
they look like they understand.

Best wishes,
Stephen Cuellca
English Language Instructor

P.S. It's not true that the Japanese don't stutter.
Because I know one who does. It sounds like
stuttering. (in both Japanese and English) SC

Postcard — S. K. List

27 JANUARY 1983

Dear Tom —
Here's another rule of thumb:
A wiener schnitzel is properly
cooked if you can sit on it quickly
and not leave a stain on your good
trousers.

S. K. List
2413 Mecklenburg Rd.
RD3
Trumansburg, NY 14886

Postcard — R. Buckminster Fuller

1. "WHEN IN DOUBT, DON'T"
2. ALL "SOMETHINGS" OR "THOUGHTS" ARE SYSTEMS. SYSTEMS ALWAYS DIVIDE THE WHOLE UNIVERSE INTO ALL THE MACROCOSM IRRELEVANTLY SURROUNDING THE SYSTEM AND ALL THE MICRO IRRELEVANCIES INSIDE THE SYSTEM AND THE REMAINDER OF UNIVERSE WHICH IS THE CONSIDERED SYSTEM DOING THE DIVIDING.
3. THE NUMBER OF INTERRELATIONSHIPS OF A GIVEN NUMBER OF SYSTEMS IS ALWAYS N^2-N
4. ONE MINUTE OF LONGITUDE IS ONE NAUTICAL MILE.
5. IF ANOTHER MOVING OBJECT MAINTAINS SAME ANGLE RELATIVE TO YOUR COURSE, YOU ARE COLLISION BOUND.

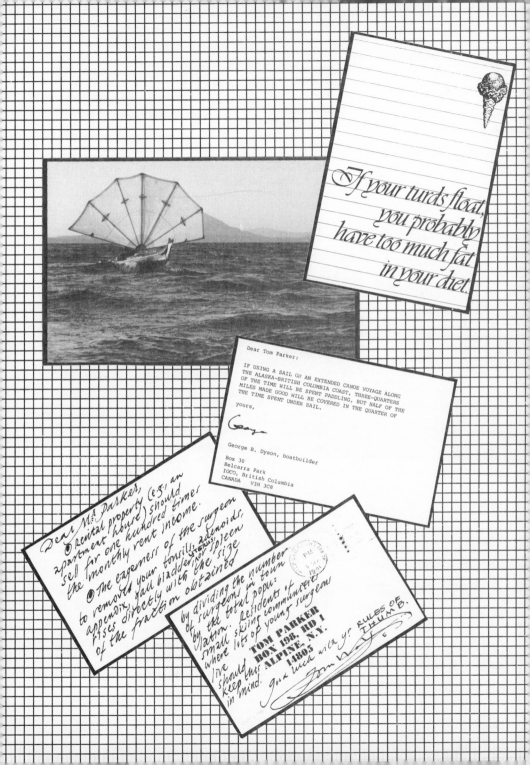

If your turds float, you probably have too much fat in your diet.

Dear Tom Parker:

IF USING A SAIL ON AN EXTENDED CANOE VOYAGE ALONG THE ALASKA-BRITISH COLUMBIA COAST, THREE-QUARTERS OF THE TIME WILL BE SPENT PADDLING, BUT HALF OF THE MILES MADE GOOD WILL BE COVERED IN THE QUARTER OF THE TIME SPENT UNDER SAIL.

yours,

George

George B. Dyson, boatbuilder

Box 30
Belcarra Park
IOCO, British Columbia
CANADA   V3H 3C8

Dear Mr. Parker,
① Rental property (e.g. an apartment house) should sell for one hundred times the monthly rent income.
② The eagerness of the surgeon to remove your tonsils, adenoids, appendix, gall bladder, uterus, spleen rises directly with the size of the fraction obtained

by dividing the number of surgeons in town by the total population. Residents of small skiing communities where lots of young surgeons live should keep this in mind.

Good luck with yr. RULES OF THUMB.

TOM PARKER
BOX 198, RD I
ALPINE, N.Y.
14805

Tom K

84. STORMS IN THE MIDWEST In the midwestern states, only one storm in ten comes from the northwest. These storms are bad ones — bad thunderstorms in the summer, bad blizzards in the winter. *Glenn Saha, builder*

85. WAITING FOR A CHANCE TO SAY SOMETHING People will lapse into silence after every twenty minutes of conversation. *Margie Halpin, unemployed sprinkler fitter's apprentice, Cincinnati, Ohio*

86. MAKING A SCARF JOINT Two pieces of wood can be attached end to end by tapering each piece and overlapping the tapers. The splice that is formed is called a scarf joint. For planking a boat, the length of the tapers should be twelve times the thickness of the boards being joined. *Larry Beck, joiner*

87. BUYING AN ENGINE If you are checking out a used engine that doesn't run, ignore the cleanliness of the outside and look into the carburetor throat. If it is stained reddish brown, chances are good that the engine has been well cared for. A black stain below the choke butterfly is an indication of a tired engine. *LeRoi Smith, writer and car builder*

88. LOOKING FOR MUSHROOMS Look for morel mushrooms when the apple trees are blooming. *John Schubert, editor, Bicycling magazine*

89. COOKING SPAGHETTI When spaghetti is done, it will stick to the wall. *Numerous students*

90. RENOVATING A LARGE BUILDING Renovation generally saves only 10 to 15 percent of the cost of new construction. *James Colby, civil engineer*

91. AVOIDING OTHER AIRPLANES If you spot another airplane and it is above the horizon, it is above you. If it is below the horizon, it is below you. If the other airplane is at the same level as the horizon, it is at your altitude. If an approaching airplane appears motionless, it is on a collision course with you. *John Stickle, flight instructor*

92. MEASURING LONGITUDE One minute of longitude is one nautical mile. *R. Buckminster Fuller, architect and inventor of the geodesic dome*

93. TIMING YOUR IGNITION You can set your ignition timing very nicely by testing it on the road. Slowly advance the distributor until a slight ping can be heard when the throttle is suddenly opened at thirty miles per hour in high gear. Then retard the distributor just a bit until the ping disappears. This setting will be close to perfect.
LeRoi Smith, writer and car builder

94. PLACING AN AD IN A MAGAZINE   The first right-hand page and the back cover are usually the best place for advertisements. These are followed by the other cover positions and the front section of the magazine. Unless you run your ad in a mail-order section, positions in the back of the magazine usually produce a much lower response.
Jim Kobs, Kobs and Brady Advertising, Chicago, Illinois

95. ESTIMATING MATERIALS   For standard residential construction with wall studs on 16-inch centers, plan on using one stud per linear foot of wall plus two per opening and you'll be pretty close.
Jim Underwood, Technology Center for Mountain People, Cherry Grove, West Virginia

96. POLITICAL CAMPAIGNS   A certain percentage of voters will be for or against you based purely on party affiliation. Only a small percentage of voters are truly independent and will consider you without bias. (See your local political hack to fill in the percentages on this one; it varies widely by district.)
Tom Wilbur, county commissioner, East Lansing, Michigan

97. WEANING A CALF   Wean a calf when it has gained fifteen pounds over its birth weight.
Edward Dalrymple, dairy farmer

98. WEANING A CALF   Wean a calf when it consumes more than a pound of grain a day on a regular basis.
John C. Porter, cooperative extension agent

99. PLANNING A RACING SEASON   Planning a racing season is a matter of setting some goals. You will be giving yourself a sensible target if you aim for 65-percent reliability, starting in the front half of the grid, and finishing with the first six cars.
Frank Gardner, 1972–73 British Driving Champion

100. BUYING BATTERIES   In most cases a lithium battery will last as long as four alkaline batteries and an alkaline battery will last as long as ten carbon-zinc batteries.   *W. Price, transistor radio lover*

101. CAVING WITH BEGINNERS There should be at least one experienced caver for every three beginners. However, never have less than two experienced cavers on any trip with beginners, so one can lead and one can bring up the rear.
David R. McClurg, speleologist

102. PLAYING POKER Don't enter a poker game unless you have forty times the betting limit in your pocket. If you plan to play poker for a living, start with a bankroll at least two hundred times the maximum bet. *Edwin Silberstang, games expert*

103. PLAYING POKER Don't enter a poker game unless you have sixty times the betting limit in your pocket. When you have doubled this amount, it is time to quit for the day. *John Scarne, gambling authority*

104. SAVING HEAT IN THE HOME You should try to keep heat losses from your house down to five BTUs per square foot per degree day. You can do this by putting 12 inches of insulation in your attic, 6 inches in your walls, and adding weather-tight windows and doors. *C. C. Murphy, heating consultant*

105. PASSING OUT WORK Don't give an employee a project after 4:30 unless it can be completed by 5:00. *Caroline Eckstrom, managing editor*

106. ERECTING A TELEPHONE POLE One fifth of the length of a telephone pole should be planted in the ground.
Ron Bean, mechanics of materials student, Madison, Wisconsin

107. BUILDING WITH TUBING A hollow tube should have a wall thickness that is at least one fiftieth of the tube's diameter. If the wall thickness is less, the tube won't work as a structural member — it will crumple like a beer can.
John Schubert, editor, Bicycling magazine

108. DESIGNING A COMPUTER SYSTEM
Making a design change when a computer system is nearly complete will cost about ten times as much as making the change before the work has started.
Clifton Royston, programmer/analyst, Nukualofa, Tonga

109. TYPING   Two handwritten pages equals one typed page.
Carl Mitcham, philosophy teacher, Brooklyn, New York

110. CRACKING YOUR KNUCKLES   After cracking your knuckles, it takes thirty minutes for the vaporized joint fluid to go back into solution, which it must do before you can crack them again.
Jim Crissman, veterinary pathologist, Cornell University

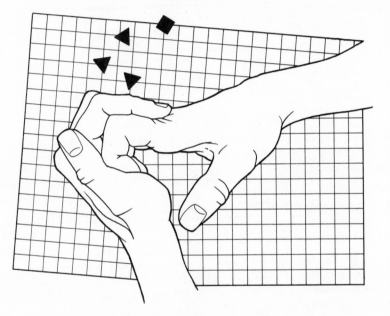

111. CALLING IN SICK   In half of all cases, when an employee calls in sick, he's actually sick.
Walter Pitkin, literary agent

112. PUBLISHING A MAGAZINE   A magazine or newspaper needs to be about 50 percent advertising to survive financially.
John Schubert, editor, Bicycling magazine

113. WRITING A FINAL SENTENCE   When writing, if you're searching for a final sentence, you've probably already written it.   *Cheryl Russell, demographer*

114. BUYING A REFRIGERATOR-FREEZER It will save you money if you buy the right size refrigerator-freezer for your family. You need a total of 8 cubic feet of space for two people, plus 1 foot for each additional family member. *Jill Phillips, home economist*

115. WATCHING SUNSETS A red sky at sunset means that wind is on the way. *Rose Bowen, seamstress*

116. MAINTAINING YOUR WEIGHT You can estimate the approximate number of calories it takes to maintain your weight by multiplying your current weight by fifteen. To lose or gain weight, alter your calorie intake by 20 percent in the desired direction. *F. Jill Charboneau, editor*

117. MEDICAL EMERGENCIES Sometimes a tube down the throat is used to restore free breathing. For an emergency guess, the diameter of a child's smallest finger is about the diameter of the largest endotracheal tube that he or she can be intubated with. *The Blossoms, Fresno, California*

118. FOLLOWING SPRING Spring moves north about thirteen miles a day. *Jon Reis, photographer*

119. GIVING YOUR AGE Odd-numbered ages seem older and more worldly-wise than even-numbered ages. *Hamilton Pike, Richmond, Indiana*

120. TESTING AN EDGE You can test the edge of a blade by shaving the hairs on your forearm. A knife is as sharp as it can possibly be if the hairs seem to actually pop at the touch of the blade. *D. Petzel, editor, Mechanix Illustrated magazine*

121. TESTING AN EDGE You can test the edge of a blade by running it lightly across the flat of your thumbnail. If the blade slides easily, it is dull. A sharp edge catches and digs in. *Lester McCann, Chicago, Illinois*

122. TESTING AN EDGE Any cutting edge that reflects light, from a razor blade to a chainsaw tooth, is in need of sharpening. *Michael Mangan, stained-glass designer, Carrollton, Ohio*

123. SEX IN THE CLASSROOM A computer science class will be about one-third female. A math class will be about one-tenth female.
Janet Blumer, math grad student, Denver, Colorado

124. MAKING WINE One ton of grapes will make 170 gallons of wine.
L. Wagner, vintner

125. ICE SKATING You need to have three consecutive days of sub-20-degree weather before a pond will be safe for skating. *Holley Bailey, editor*

126. COOKING OUTDOORS Melting snow for water or cooking outside a tent requires twice as much fuel as cooking inside a tent.
Peggy Kerber, editor, Mountaineering

127. SERVING SHRIMP For three servings you need one pound of shrimp in the shell or half a pound of cooked shrimp without the shell. *The Joy of Cooking*

128. EATING SHRIMP One pound of unpeeled shrimp is usually more than one person can eat.
Pamela Monell, computer programmer

129. FIXING UP OLD CARS As a rule, the average old-car enthusiast can fix up a car to rate about 75 on a scale of 100 points for perfection. Restoring a car as an investment is another matter. A high-dollar car needs to rate a 99 or 100.
LeRoi Smith, writer and car builder

130. LOSING HAIR Normal daily hair loss is one hundred to two hundred hairs per day.
Dr. Jonathan Zizmor, hair expert

131. MAKING A DOCUMENTARY FILM Most documentary film makers plan on shooting ten times the footage that will end up in the finished film.
Sandra A. Kraft, writer

132. PLANTING A BULB If you're not sure how deep to plant a flower bulb, try three times its length.
Kevin Kelly, Athens, Georgia

133. CASTING METAL   Molten metal shrinks in all directions when poured into a mold. Iron will shrink about ¹⁄₁₆ inch per foot. Aluminum will shrink about ⅛ inch per foot.   *Richard Spencer, Elmira, New York*

134. DESIGNING AN OFFICE BUILDING   A well-planned office building should be able to accommodate one person for every 225 square feet of floor space.   *William Payne, building supervisor*

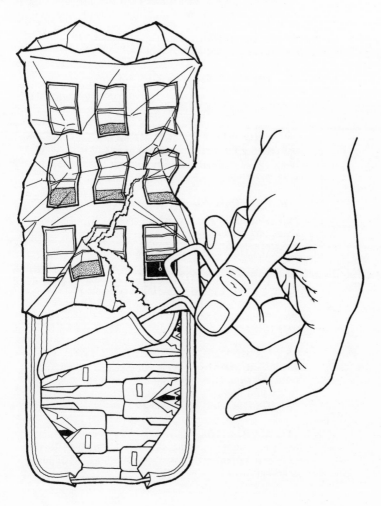

135. SCUBA DIVING The average scuba tank will provide air for forty-five minutes in 30 feet of water.
Jack T. Marshall, professional diving instructor, Trumansburg, New York

136. BUILDING A POND An earthen dam should never slope more than 1 foot in 3.
J. P. Hunter, retired engineer

137. SHOOTING AT DUCKS If you are shooting at ducks over decoys you should figure your lead, then double it before firing. If you are pass-shooting at birds without decoys, quadruple your lead.
Herman Klein, duck hunter

138. BUYING USED TOOLS A used power or hand tool in good condition should cost no more than half the price of a new one. *Mark Garner, builder*

139. CHOOSING A FACE MASK A face mask for skin diving fits properly if you can hold it on your face, out of the water, with nothing but the suction from your nose. *Dorothy Hooker, Hollywood, Florida*

140. STOCKING A TROUT POND A healthy trout pond should be stocked with three hundred fingerling trout per acre per year.
Cornell University

141. FLOWER SHOPS A flower shop or plant store should plan on spending 2 percent of its gross sales on advertising.
Bram Cavin, florist, How to Run a Successful Florist and Plant Store

142. CABINETMAKING RULE OF TWO When estimating your labor for a cabinetmaking job, compute the time it would take if everything went perfectly and multiply it by two.
Pierre Gremaud, Waitsfield, Vermont

143. MAIL-ORDER SALES The best months to sell something by mail-order are September, November, and January. Of those, September and January are best.
L. Perry Wilbur, mail-order expert, Money in Your Mailbox

144. BUYING A HORSE As far as price is concerned, the best time of year to buy a horse is fall.
Jeanne K. Posey, horse show judge

145. SELLING ANTIQUES As a rule, people don't buy antiques at Christmas time.
Dean Miller, antique dealer

146. WRITING The greater the sense of exultation and accomplishment upon completing the first draft of a work of fiction, the greater the need for revision.
James McConkey, writer, Trumansburg, New York

147. DESIGNING A COMPUTER SYSTEM For every two days spent designing a computer system, figure one day for coding or writing the programs and three days testing them.
John M. Howe (quoting Edward Brooks), North Quincy, Massachusetts

148. CHOOSING A CROSS-COUNTRY SKI POLE You can size a ski pole by standing with one arm held straight out from your side at shoulder height. A cross-country ski pole is the right length for you if it fits comfortably between the floor and your armpit.
Donald Page, chemist

149. USING A MOVIE CAMERA Count at least ten seconds every time you press a movie camera's start button. The biggest single error that novice film makers make is taking many shots in very short spurts.
Flip Schulke, underwater photographer

150. WALKING Without a pack, you should be able to walk twenty-five miles a day without serious strain. With a pack one-fourth your weight or less, fifteen miles a day is reasonable on a decent trail.
J. Baldwin, designer, writer

151. TRAVELING BY BICYCLE On a good ten-speed bicycle you can travel fifty miles per day at a leisurely pace. Riding straight through with only a few rest stops can get you seventy to eighty miles per day with little effort.
Alwyn T. Perrin, Explorers Ltd. Source Book

152. ENTERING A CONTEST If a contest calls for "twenty-five words or less," try to use as close to twenty-five words as possible. Never use less than fifteen words. *Allen Glasser, contest expert*

153. GROWING CITRUS FRUITS A freeze will destroy a citrus crop. If the temperature in a citrus grove drops to 28 degrees Fahrenheit or less before 10 P.M., fire up the smudgepots.
Darryl Payne, orange grower

154. RECOGNIZING THE OBVIOUS As a rule, clients will recognize the obvious much sooner than professionals. *Dr. Larry R. Hunt, Toronto, Ontario*

155. DEALING WITH DOUBT (EDITING)
When in doubt, cross it out.
Bryant Robey, editor, American Demographics magazine

156. COOKING WITH FIRE When cooking with an open fire, use flames for boiling and baking, coals for broiling and frying.
Larry Dean Olsen, survival instructor, Outdoor Survival Skills

157. LOSING WEIGHT A woman should not diet below an intake of 1200 calories a day; a man, below 1600 calories.
Jean Mayer, nutritionist, and Jean Goldberg, journalist

158. SHOOTING AT HELICOPTERS North Vietnamese ground troops used their thumbs to determine whether they could reach enemy aircraft with hand-held weapons. If an airplane or helicopter was bigger than a thumb held at arm's length, they could bring it down with ground fire. *D. Tanner, Fort Wayne, Indiana*

159. BUYING SODA FROM A MACHINE If your money falls right through a soft drink machine and lands in the coin return, forget about feeding it coins and try pulling a bottle out of the machine. The chances are about one in five that you will get a free soda. Someone else put money in the machine, but the relay didn't release the bottles until after they gave up and left.
Eric Kimple, motorcycle racer, Columbus, Ohio

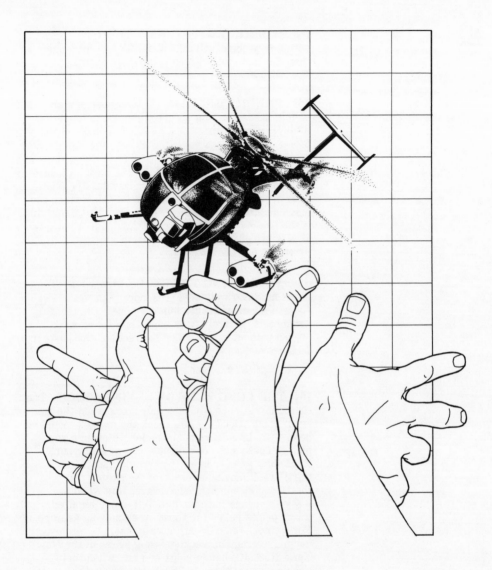

160. WORKING WITH A NEW CLIENT A job
with a new client will take about 25 percent longer
than the same job with an established client.
Mike Rider, art director

161. PREDICTING RAIN The number of stars
visible inside the ring around the moon is the number
of days before rain.
Glenn Saha, builder

162. FINDING DIRECTIONS The bark on a dead
tree holds moisture on the northern side. For this
reason, the tree is usually wet under the bark on the
north side, while the other side is dry. This damp side
is the first to rot. The center of the damp or rotten
area is usually slightly east of north.
Alwyn T. Perrin, editor, Explorers Ltd. Source Book

163. FOLLOWING THE STOCK MARKET The
stock market rarely advances more than ten or twelve
days in a row without a minor setback. On a longer-
term basis, it rarely rises more than six or seven
weeks without a setback or "correction" that lasts two
to four weeks.
Boardroom Reports

164. THE LONG RULE OF BUYING STOCK The
classic investment advice is: buy stock when the market is weak. Deciding how weak the market should be
before you buy depends on the length of time you
plan to hold your stock. If you plan to keep your
stock for a year or more, you should maintain a
thirty-week moving average of the closing prices of
the Dow Jones industrial average. Buy when the
weekly average falls one hundred to one hundred
thirty points below the thirty-week moving average.
For a three- to six-month investment, use a ten-week
moving average of weekly closing prices of the New
York Stock Exchange index and buy when the weekly
closing price is three to four points below the moving
average. For investments lasting less than three
months, use a ten-day moving average of the daily
closing prices of the NYSE index and buy when the
index falls two to three points below the moving average. *Boardroom Reports*

165. TUNING A MUSICAL INSTRUMENT A stringed instrument is less apt to slip out of pitch if the strings are tuned up from flat than it is if the strings are tuned down from sharp.
Robbie Aceto, musician

166. TRAVELING IN LOS ANGELES In an L. A. rapid transit bus with four-across seating, never stand or sit more than 6 feet from the nearest exit unless you're planning to ride all the way to the end of the line. This rule still applies if you are getting off one stop from the end.
Timothy Horrigan, Los Angeles, California

167. TRAVELING IN MASSACHUSETTS When you are trying to get somewhere in Boston without directions, take a turn at every major intersection — never go straight. When you are trying to do the same on Cape Cod, never turn — always go straight and look for the signs.
David Notkin, Pittsburgh, Pennsylvania

168. COMING UP WITH IDEAS New idea meetings need five people, and preferably twelve. Mix ages and backgrounds. When the group runs dry, re-state the problem. At the end, go back to the wildest two ideas and see what innovations they inspire.
J. Geoffrey Rawlinson, Creative Thinking and Brainstorming

169. HEAT LOST THROUGH THE ROOF If the coldest temperature in your attic is within one or two degrees Fahrenheit of the coldest temperature outdoors, your ceiling is fairly well insulated.
Steven Flood, Saginaw, Michigan

170. TREATING SERIOUS BURNS Add a burn victim's age to the percent of their body covered with second- or third-degree burns. If the sum is less than one hundred, the patient is apt to survive.
Gerald Myers, Redway, California

171. INVITING GUESTS If you invite one hundred people to a cocktail party, plan on seventy-five coming; twenty-five will send regrets.
Alan Amsler, graphic designer

172. BUYING A COMPUTER A computer system capable of doing record-keeping and accounting for a business should cost 1 to 2 percent of the company's annual sales.   *The Business Automation Bulletin, Phoenix, Arizona*

173. FATTENING A BEEF COW To fatten a beef for slaughter, feed it one pound of grain per day per one hundred pounds of weight.
George Bernius, Cincinnati, Ohio

174. BUTCHERING BEEF You are doing O.K. if you get half a beef cow's live weight in usable meat.
Ken Leach, meat cutter

175. PETTING A HORSE Rub a horse's face and ears as gently as you would pet a cat.
Stacey DiGiovani, equestrian

176. HANDLING TEST EQUIPMENT Don't tap the face of a sticky gauge any harder than you would tap the bridge of your nose.
Steve Parker, aerospace engineer, Princeton, New Jersey

177. ABSORBING ALCOHOL Traces of alcohol remain in the body for forty-eight hours.
Whetstone, Lafayette, Louisiana

178. DIGESTING A MEAL As a rule, it will take forty-eight hours to completely digest a meal.
Stephen Flanders, Princeton, New Jersey

179. TREATING MUNICIPAL SEWAGE You can plan on one-fifth of a pound (dry weight) of body waste per person. Anaerobic digestion of a pound of this material produces 18 cubic feet of gas with a heat value of 650 BTUs per cubic foot.
Dan Cortinovis, sanitary engineer, Lafayette, California

180. CRASHING AN AIRPLANE Three acts of poor judgment equals one airplane accident.
Jim Corey, airport administrator

181. SPONSORING LARGE SPORTS EVENTS
There aren't any precise studies showing what sponsorship is worth, but the rule of thumb is that putting $1000 behind a sports event will generate the same exposure as $10,000 in advertising.
The Wall Street Journal

182. JUDGING ADS FOR HORSES Any mention of horse shows in an advertisement for a horse generally indicates that the horse is pleasing to look at. If training or manners are emphasized and looks are not mentioned, the horse is probably not particularly handsome. A poorly written ad that leaves out vital statistics will generally lead to a mediocre horse.
Jeanne K. Posey, horse show judge

183. ESTIMATING THE SIZE OF YOUR FOOT
The distance from your elbow to your wrist equals the length of your foot.
Carla Corin, biologist, Eagles River, Alaska

184. BUILDING STAIRS A staircase will be pleasant to use if the height of one step (the riser) multiplied by the width of one tread equals 70 to 75 inches.
Stephen Gibian, architect and stonemason

185. BUILDING STAIRS A set of steps will be comfortable to use if two times the height of one riser, plus the width of one tread is equal to twenty-six inches.
Alice Lukens Bachelder, gardener, San Anselmo, California

186. BUILDING STAIRS A set of steps will be comfortable to use if two times the height of one riser, plus the width of one tread is equal to twenty-five inches.
Ken Vineberg, architect

187. BUILDING STAIRS Build steps that are 7 inches high and 10 inches wide.
Harry Pate, builder, Camden, New Jersey

188. CHOOSING AN ICE AX An ice ax, standard equipment for climbing on snow or ice, should reach from your wrist to the ground with your arms at your sides.
R. Maynard, Fullerton, California

189. SAILING When the ship's bell rings on its own, it is past time to reef your sail.
Gary Closter, sailor

190. PLANNING A KITCHEN Plan about 12 square feet of cupboard space for glassware and china and an additional 6 square feet per family member for general storage. *Marcia Southwick, writer and builder*

191. GETTING TO KNOW PEOPLE Everyone knows at least 250 people well enough to invite to their wedding or funeral.
Joe Girard, "world's greatest salesman"

192. DIGGING A GRAVE When digging a grave by hand, haul away seventeen wheelbarrow loads of dirt and pile the rest by the hole. You will have just the right amount to backfill.
Randall Lacey, wind-power engineer

193. PUBLISHING A BOOK You can hype a book by a famous author to 250,000 copies. After that, success or failure depends upon word of mouth.
John Gill, publisher

194. MAKING WIGS Dark hair bleaches whiter than blond hair, so as a rule, the best white hair for making wigs comes from the countries that have the best dark hair. *Meg Wallace, counselor*

195. USING A ROPE If you are using a rope with a knot or a sharp bend, you should assume that its strength is reduced by 50 percent.
Frank Potts, Salem, Oregon

196. BRITISH THERMAL UNITS One BTU is roughly equal to the amount of heat energy given off by burning a wooden kitchen match.
Robert G. Flower, engineer

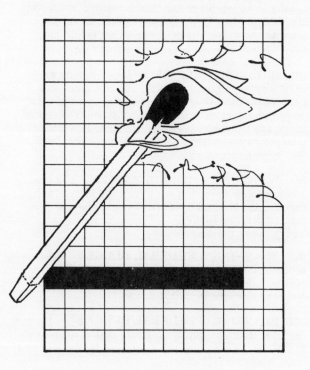

197. SAVING MONEY You should have six months' salary in savings for emergencies.
Bob Horton, statistics consultant, West Lafayette, Indiana

198. DELEGATING AUTHORITY I make it an absolute rule not to make decisions that somebody else can make. The first rule of leadership is to save yourself for the big decisions. *Richard M. Nixon, former president of the United States, as quoted in Time magazine*

199. CHECKING A SICK ENGINE The first step in checking a sick racing engine is to haul off the oil filters and examine them for traces of metal. It is time to start worrying when you start finding shavings more than a ¼ inch long. If you find bits of white metal with brass attached, it is time to start checking your bank account.
Frank Gardner, 1972–73 British Driving Champion

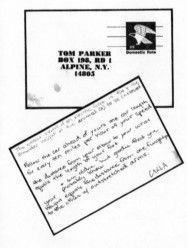

TOM PARKER
BOX 198, RD 1
ALPINE, N.Y.
14805

Domestic Rate

200. DIVING RULE OF TWO The height of a cliff usually looks much greater than it really is when you are about to dive off it. To estimate the actual distance to the water, divide the apparent height by two. *John Lilly, mechanical engineer and cliff diver*

201. BUILDING RULE OF TWO If you are an amateur and you want to figure out how much it is going to cost you to build a house, add up all of your projected expenses, then multiply by two. The second figure will be much closer than the first. It will also take you twice as long to build it as you think it will.
Carl Mitcham, philosophy teacher, Brooklyn, New York

202. WATCHING A THUNDERSTORM You can tell how many miles you are from a thunderstorm by counting the seconds between the lightning and thunder and dividing by five.
Millie Stoerdeur, Cincinnati, Ohio

203. PLANNING A FEDERAL BUDGET A 1-percent rise in the unemployment rate adds $5 billion a year to federal spending.
Jonathan Fuerbringer, The New York Times

204. PLANNING A FEDERAL BUDGET A 1-percent rise in the unemployment rate cuts revenues by $12 billion a year. *Jonathan Fuerbringer, The New York Times*

205. PLANNING A FEDERAL BUDGET A 1-percent increase in the inflation rate over what a budget was initially based on adds about $5 billion of revenue in the first year. *Jonathan Fuerbringer, The New York Times*

206. PLANNING A FEDERAL BUDGET A 1-percent rise in the inflation rate will add $1.3 billion to federal spending in the first year.
Jonathan Fuerbringer, The New York Times

207. PLANNING A FEDERAL BUDGET A 1-percent rise in interest rates adds $2.3 billion a year to federal spending.
Jonathan Fuerbringer, The New York Times

208. WAITING FOR WIND When you are sailing on a lake you should allow for a one-hour period of calm starting thirty minutes before sunset.
Joe Hlebica, Tokyo, Japan

209. SHAVING Your face is dry and puffy when you first wake up. Put off shaving two minutes for each hour you slept. *E. L. Beck, Orlando, Florida*

210. HAVING YOUR CAR FIXED Any time a mechanic starts a conversation by telling you how lucky you are that you brought your car in when you did, plan on spending at least $100.
Carl Frandsen, Trumansburg, New York

211. RENTING A TUXEDO Tuxedos last a long time and rarely go out of style. If you need to wear one even once a year, it pays to buy and avoid the ordeal of renting. *Doug Weaver, accountant*

212. ADAPTING A NOVEL FOR FILM As a rule, the more you liked the novel, the less you will like the movie that is made from it.
Rebecca Sawyer, bookkeeper

213. MOVIE SEQUELS As a rule, if you didn't care for the original movie, you will like the sequel even less. *A wandering moviegoer, Oklahoma City, Oklahoma*

214. SWIMMING Swimming a quarter of a mile is roughly equal to running one mile.
Cynthia Gaines, photographer

215. LOGGING For some reason, most serious sawing accidents happen to beginners or to professionals in their eighth year of logging.
Ned Bounds, sawyer, Salmon, Idaho

216. FEEDING LIVESTOCK Two heifers eat as much as one cow; one cow eats as much as seven sheep. *Monica Crispin, cooperative extension agent*

217. CHOOSING A WOODSTOVE If you are trying to decide what size woodstove you need you can start by figuring 2.5 cubic feet of firebox per 1000 square feet of living space.
Dan Hoffman, city council alderman

218. WATCHING THE PRICE OF OIL A change of $1 per barrel in the price of crude oil means a change of 2.5¢ per gallon in the price of gasoline.
Mike Rider, art director

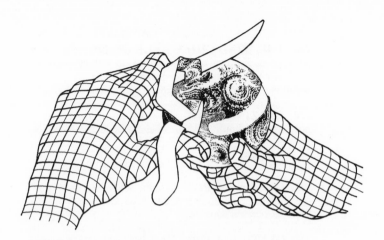

219. READING A MAP You can tell where a map of the world was made by seeing which country is smack dab in the middle.
Adham Loutfi, Oakland, California

220. USING HERBS AND SPICES When using a recipe, double the amount of herbs and spices called for, and quadruple the onions and garlic.
Stephanie Mills, writer

221. MANAGING A WOOD LOT A properly managed wood lot in a good location will produce about two-thirds of a cord of hardwood per acre per year. A ten- to twelve-acre wood lot can easily meet the heating needs of the average, well-insulated house.
Gary Goff, extension forester

222. READING RUSSIAN Whenever *Pravda* or a Soviet spokesperson begins a statement with the words "As is well known . . .," you should question the rest of the sentence. *Walter Pitkin, literary agent*

223. SCUBA DIVING A scuba diver should never ascend faster than 60 feet per minute.
Jack T. Marshall, professional diving instructor, Trumansburg, New York

224. FINDING INTERRELATIONSHIPS The number of interrelationships in a given number of systems is always N^2-N divided by 2.
R. Buckminster Fuller, architect and inventor of the geodesic dome

225. THE WIND CHILL RULE OF THIRTY At 30 degrees Fahrenheit below zero, in a thirty-mile-per-hour wind, exposed flesh freezes in thirty seconds. *Lory Peck, social activist*

226. GLAZING A POT In order to properly coat a pot, a glaze should be the consistency of heavy whipping cream.
M. N., Enterprise, Oregon

227. GLAZING A POT Hold a pot in the glaze for the time it takes your heart to beat four times.
Kathy Edmondson, potter

228. GETTING A JOB Most job seekers can expect one to five job leads and/or interviews for every one hundred résumés they mail out.
Karen E. O'Neill, career consultant, Englewood, Colorado

229. PLANNING A FLIGHT Add half a gallon of fuel per cylinder to normal fuel consumption to determine the climb fuel for a normally aspirated light airplane. Also add a couple of gallons for taxi and takeoff. *Bruce Landsberg, pilot and writer*

230. PLANNING A FLIGHT A fuel stop will add forty-five minutes to the total trip time. The average fuel stop includes personal refreshment, at least one phone call, paying the fuel bill, and a walk around to check fuel caps and sumps. Add ten minutes if a squall line is approaching and you are hoping to depart before the weather arrives.
Bruce Landsberg, pilot and writer

231. SLOPING SEWER PIPES Sewage flows best in a pipe that is sloped a ¼ inch per foot. If the pitch is too steep, the liquid runs off and leaves the solids behind; too shallow, and nothing runs at all.
Raleigh Fillings, plumber

232. PLAYING THE GOLD MARKET In the gold market, if the public is selling, buy. If the public is buying, sell. *J. Snyder, credit manager*

233. MAKING CANDLES One pound of wax will make eight 8-inch candles. *Nancy Heffernan Eckstrom, dietician*

234. PHOTOGRAPHING A CAR   A three-quarter front view makes the most effective photograph for selling a car.   *Paul Douglas, photographer*

235. AIMING A SOLAR WATER HEATER   For year-round use, the slope of home hot water solar collectors should be equal to the latitude at which they are installed.
Stephen Gibian, architect and stonemason, Ithaca, New York

236. BOILING WATER AWAY   Changing boiling water to vapor takes about six times the energy needed to raise the same amount of water from freezing to boiling.   *John Hollowell, cook*

237. FUELING A HOT AIR BALLOON   You get about half an hour of flight in a hot air balloon per twenty-pound tank of propane gas.
Barbara Frederking, balloonist

238. ARRANGING FLOWERS   A flower arrangement should usually be about one and a half times the height or width of the container.   *Pamela Reeger, florist*

239. GROWING YOUR OWN HERBS   If you are setting aside space to grow herbs for your own family, figure 2 square feet for each variety you plan to grow.   *Jean Moses, Lincoln, Nebraska*

240. BUYING CAR INSURANCE   If your car is worth $1500 or more, you should carry collision insurance. However, you can save money by choosing a policy with a higher deductible. As a rule, your collision deductible should equal one week's take-home pay.   *Paul Majka, author, You Can Save a Bundle on Your Car Insurance*

241. PUBLIC SPEAKING   Address your lecture to the median intelligence of your audience.
Carla van Berkum, Russian studies teacher, Baltimore, Maryland

242. BUYING A CAR   When you buy a used car, replace all of its fluids, even the brake fluid. The water that accumulates in old fluid will slowly rust the parts that it touches.
Al Kaehler, mechanical engineer, Mountain View, California

243. HITCHHIKING   The more graffiti there is on the back of a road sign, the harder it will be to hitch a ride standing next to it.
John Gize, reprobate, Calgary, Alberta

244. BUYING A CAR STEREO   Strictly speaking, the sound you hear from a car stereo system is made by the speakers, not the radio/tape deck. According to some experts, if your speakers cost less than two-thirds of the price of your radio/tape deck, you're not putting the deck to good use.
Chas. Turner, Rockford, Illinois

245. MAKING MILK   A cow needs about three pounds of water to make a pound of milk.
Monica Crispin, cooperative extension agent

246. POLITICAL CAMPAIGNS   When you are canvassing door-to-door you can optimize your "time per voter" by spending no more than twenty to thirty seconds with each person you meet. Most people will decide whether they like you within that time and most will want to get back to whatever they were doing when you interrupted them. You should, however, take time to discuss issues with the interested persons.
Tom Wilbur, county commissioner, East Lansing, Michigan

247. POLITICAL CAMPAIGNS   Candidates with strong, aggressive personalities, and "programs" to sell get elected half as often and last half as long as accommodating, compromising candidates who are interesting persons and want to provide "constituent services."
Tom Wilbur, county commissioner, East Lansing, Michigan

248. POLITICAL CAMPAIGNS   For every person who gets involved in your campaign by contributing money, putting up a lawn sign, distributing literature, or signing an endorsement letter, expect ten to fifteen votes on election day.
Tom Wilbur, county commissioner, East Lansing, Michigan

249. POLITICAL CAMPAIGNS   While money doesn't guarantee a victory, the lack of money guarantees a loss.   *Neil Wallace, unsuccessful congressional campaigner*

250. WALKING ON ICE On snow-covered ice, stay away from areas without snow. This could be a sign of thin ice that has only recently frozen.
Jim Keneely, professional guide

251. GETTING EMOTIONALLY INVOLVED
Wait at least a year after a divorce before becoming emotionally committed to someone else. Some psychologists say that a person needs one year to resolve a divorce for every five years of marriage.
Corinne Abbott, Manitou Springs, Colorado

252. CONSULTING A consultant should never charge for less than half a day of work.
Daniel Corbitt, consultant

253. CHECKING A BRINE SOLUTION A 10-percent brine solution will float a two-ounce egg so the shell just breaks the surface of the liquid.
The Joy of Cooking

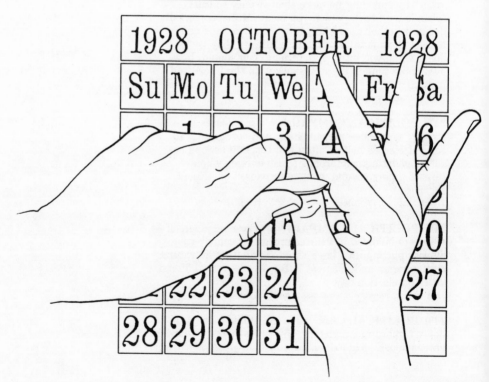

254. CHECKING AN EGG   When placed in a bowl of water, a fresh egg will sink and lie on its side. An egg that's not fresh but still edible will sink and stand partially erect on its tapered end. A rotten egg will float.
David Hechler, writer, Rockport, Texas

255. CATCHING A SWARM OF BEES   A swarm of bees in May is worth a load of hay; a swarm of bees in June is worth a silver spoon; a swarm of bees in July is hardly worth a fly.
Otis Hassler, shovel operator

256. SAVING OIL RESOURCES   Every $10 you spend on conservation saves one barrel of oil.
Robert Mendenhall, Boulder, Colorado

257. PAINTING A HIGHWAY   A road must carry traffic of at least four hundred cars per day for a reflective centerline to be a cost-effective improvement.
John Schubert, editor, Bicycling magazine

258. UNDERGROUND TEMPERATURES   The internal temperature of the earth increases with depth. In most places the temperature increases about 16 degrees Fahrenheit per 1000 feet.
Steve Parker, aerospace engineer, Princeton, New Jersey

259. SHIFTING GEARS ON A BICYCLE   If the gear is too high, your legs will tire before your lungs. If the gear is too low, your lungs will tire first.
John S. Allen, author, The Complete Book of Bicycle Commuting

260. FINDING A LOW PRESSURE SYSTEM   To determine the approximate direction of the center of a low pressure system, stand with your back to the wind and your arm extended sideways. If you move your arm forward about 45 degrees, you will be pointing to the center of the low. If a low pressure system is to the west of you it often means you are in for poor weather.   *Stephen Friends, meteorologist*

261. RAISING PIGS   When a sow conceives, make a notch just above the moon on your fingernail. When this mark grows off the end of the nail, the sow is about to give birth.   *Doug Webb, Brooktondale, New York*

262. CATCHING FISH Fish are feeding actively only 5 to 10 percent of the time. The rest of the time they are either in a neutral feeding mood (80 percent) or a negative one (10 percent).
Chet Meyers and Al Lindner, fishing experts

263. FEEDING LOBSTERS Freshly caught lobsters can be kept alive in tanks if properly fed. Plan on using one bushel of fish scraps per week per 1000 pounds of lobster.
T. M. Prudden, lobster expert

264. PROOFREADING If you find one error while proofreading, there are likely to be several more in the same or contiguous paragraphs.
Cheryl Russell, demographer

265. FLYING A SAILPLANE If your tow-rope breaks below 200 feet, land straight ahead.
Tom Knauff, glider pilot

266. MEASURING SNOW One inch of rain would make ten inches of snow.
Amy Lippmann, Haifa, Israel

267. DEBUGGING COMPUTERS The number of bugs in computer software decreases exponentially with each repair, since each repair contains about the same percentage of errors as the original code.
Robert Frederking, Pittsburgh, Pennsylvania

268. SELLING THINGS BY MAIL If you get more than two replies for every hundred pieces of mail you send out, you're doing great.
Peter Francese, magazine publisher

269. SENDING CHRISTMAS CARDS You should receive at least two Christmas cards for every three you mail out. If you don't you are sending cards to the wrong people.
Shelley Mosher, Groton, New York

270. BUILDING A FIREPLACE The flue area of a fireplace should be equal to or slightly greater than one-tenth of the area of the fireplace opening.
Stephen Gibian, architect and stonemason, Ithaca, New York

271. CHANGING YOUR SEX   A sex change operation will age you five years.
A. A. Kennerly, New York City

272. BUYING LIFE INSURANCE   The average family should have life insurance coverage worth at least six times its annual income.
Stephanie Betz, accountant

273. RUNNING A CORPORATION   A corporation should limit its executive staff to one hundred people or less, even though it may have thousands of employees.   *Raymond Davies, marketing director*

274. THROWING A POT   One pound of clay thrown with reasonable competence on a potter's wheel will make a vessel large enough to hold one average serving of most kinds of food.
Jim Dunn, potter, Belews Creek, North Carolina

275. MAKING A SERVING DISH   To make a ceramic serving dish, casserole, or bean pot, use one pound of clay for each person you want the pot to serve. For example, five pounds of clay will make a dish that will serve five people, with second helpings for some.   *Jim Dunn, potter, Belews Creek, North Carolina*

276. CHECKING A BEEHIVE   One thousand to fifteen hundred bees die per day under normal summer conditions. All or most are removed from the vicinity of the hive. An accumulation of three or four dead bees per day in front of the hive entrance is cause for suspicion.   *Cornell University*

277. FISHING WITH A BAROMETER   The lower the barometer, the better the fishing.
Charles Vanderpool, Chattanooga, Tennessee

278. FIELDING A BASEBALL   A ball hit to left field by a left-handed hitter, will slice toward the left-field line. It works exactly the opposite way with a right-handed hitter.
Pete Rose, first baseman, Pete Rose's Winning Baseball

279. FINDING A MISSING PERSON   One trained dog equals sixty search-and-rescue workers.
Charles Stoehr, dog trainer, Cincinnati, Ohio

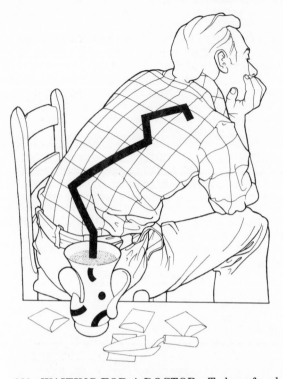

280. WAITING FOR A DOCTOR To be safe, plan on sitting around for at least half an hour on any visit to a doctor or dentist. You can save yourself time by taking the first appointment of the day or the first appointment after lunch.
Peter F. Ayer, professor of music, West Bend, Wisconsin

281. USING A TELEPHONE If a phone rings more than six times it probably won't be answered.
Cheryl Russell, demographer

282. SERVING WINE Red wines should "breathe" two minutes for every year between the vintage and the present date.
Janet Blumer, math grad student, Denver, Colorado

283. WEARING NO PANTS On a cold day, soaking wet blue jeans will draw heat from your lower body twice as fast as wearing no pants at all.
Rob Weinberg, Tassajara Zen Mountain Center, Carmel Valley, California

284. GRINDING WHEAT   One pound of wheat will make about three cups of flour.
Ronald MacInerney, Duluth, Minnesota

285. SIZING PIPE   A work-gloved hand is useful for sorting pipe. If your first two fingers slide easily into the hole, it's 1½-inch pipe. If you have to twist and force them to fit, it's 1¼ inches. For some reason, this works for small paws, gorilla mitts, and all hands in between.
Margie Halpin, unemployed sprinkler fitter's apprentice,
Cincinnati, Ohio

286. BUYING A COMPUTER   Every two years you can buy a computer that performs twice as well for half the price.
Dave KcKeown, computer scientist

287. MOVING TO A NEW HOUSE   Each time you move, things are lost, broken, or discarded. For the average family, six moves equal one house fire.
Carl Mitcham, philosophy teacher, Brooklyn, New York

288. GETTING RID OF THINGS   If you are simply trying to get rid of some unwanted household "stuff," three moves equal one house fire.
Peter Leach, potter, Dennison, Minnesota

289. MAKING AN ANIMATED MOVIE   Animated characters are more lifelike if their actions are slightly sped up.
Scott Marsh, photographer

290. FERTILIZING TREES   Most trees need about half a pound of nitrogen per inch of trunk diameter.
Shelly Wade, tree specialist

291. SELLING COLLECTIBLES   To cover costs and show a profit, try to triple your money on things that sell for less than $5 and double your money on things that sell for more than $5.
Sam Gaben, Indianapolis, Indiana

292. BURNING COAL   A pound of coal will provide slightly more than twice as much heat as a pound of wood.   *A. Alvarez, Johnstown, Pennsylvania*

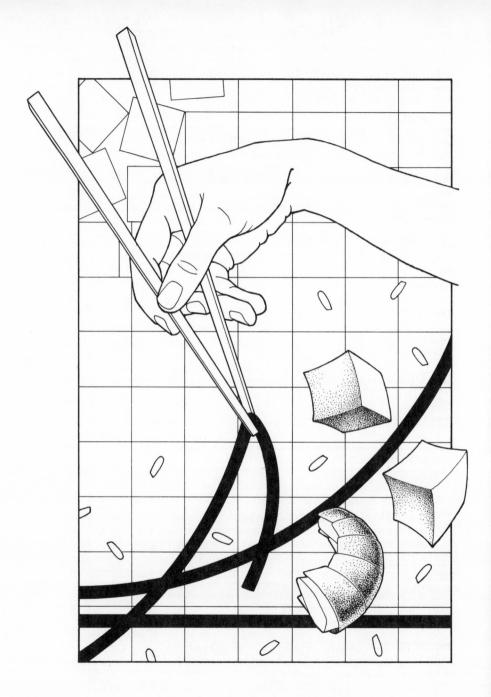

293. MAKING ELECTRICITY FROM COAL It takes about a pound of coal to produce a kilowatt-hour of electricity. Your electric bill will list the number of kilowatt hours you use every month. You can use this figure to find how much coal was burned to meet your demand for electricity. *John Kellog, electrical engineer*

294. MAKING ELECTRICITY FROM COAL How much coal do you use each year? An electric water heater uses two tons of coal for an average-size family. Electric ranges and clothes dryers use another half-ton of coal each. A color television uses about five hundred pounds of coal each year; an electric frying pan, two hundred. *John Kellog, electrical engineer*

295. TYPING A full, double-spaced typewritten page will have about 250 words on it if typed with a pica typewriter, 330 words if typed with an elite typewriter. *Michael Armstrong, writer, Anchorage, Alaska*

296. THE RESTAURANT RULE OF THREE The third restaurant to go into a space is generally the one that succeeds. *Jeff Furman, business consultant*

297. DEALING WITH DOUBT (RACE CAR ENGINES) When in doubt, whip it out. *Frank Gardner, 1972–73 British Racing Champion*

298. RUNNING A DAIRY A dairy operation uses a lot of water. You should plan on using 50 gallons of water per day for every cow in your herd. *Gary Pfaff, dairy farmer*

299. PAINTING LANDSCAPES OUTDOORS Artists who paint outdoors should assume that a dramatic effect rarely lasts more than one hour. *B. G. Truley, weekend painter*

300. DESIGNING A BROCHURE You should figure that layout and finished art for a high-quality brochure will cost you $250 per page. *Alan Amsler, graphic designer*

301. FEEDING LARGE GROUPS Three tofu buckets of chopped vegetables will feed one hundred people. *Christiann Dean, sociologist*

302. BUYING A HOUSE The first thing to check in a house is the doors and door hardware. If the doors don't fit well or the hardware is cheap and flimsy the house will be full of problems.
Walter Pitkin, literary agent

303. SNAKEHOLING A BOULDER You can blow up a boulder by digging underneath it and putting dynamite in the hole, a practice known as snakeholing. Use two sticks of dynamite for every foot the rock is thick. *Joe Kaiser, Covington, Kentucky*

304. PRODUCING FOOD WITH YOUR POND
A healthy trout pond should produce twenty to forty pounds of trout per acre per year. A bass and shiner minnow pond will produce twenty-five pounds of bass per acre per year. A bass and bluegill pond can produce fifteen pounds of bass and thirty-five pounds of bluegill per acre per year. *Cornell University*

305. MAKING GRUEL To make gruel for a baby or invalid, cook the cereal with three times the amount of water or milk called for and simmer twice as long. *The Joy of Cooking*

306. SELLING SCIENCE FICTION Science fiction books with green covers don't sell as well as those with blue covers. *Anonymous publisher*

307. MANAGING A WOOD LOT A wood lot managed primarily for saw timber will produce about four times as much money as a wood lot managed for firewood. *Gary Goff, extension forester*

308. SELLING REAL ESTATE Rental property should sell for about one hundred times its monthly rental income. *Tom Wolfe, writer*

309. JOB INTERVIEWING During a job interview, never spend more than sixty seconds answering a question. *Cheryl Russell, demographer*

310. MAIL-ORDER CATALOGUES You're not ready to publish your own mail-order catalogue until you have at least ten thousand customers.
L. Perry Wilbur, mail-order expert, Money in Your Mailbox

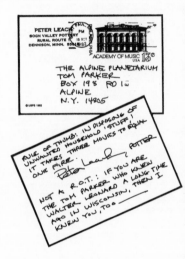

311. MONEY FOR RACING CARS Put together a budget for your first racing season, including car preparation, safety equipment, entry fees, and travel expenses, then add 50 percent to the total to come up with a realistic figure.
Alan Johnson, four-time SCCA national driving champion

312. RAISING WILD ANIMALS Keep baby animals in something that is 90 to 95 degrees Fahrenheit until their eyes open, then lower the temperature 5 degrees a week to room temperature.
Carl Grummich, veterinarian

313. USING A PILOT LIGHT Most gas ovens with a pilot light maintain a steady temperature of 90 degrees Fahrenheit when the burners are off.
Francis York, chicken farmer

314. USING DYNAMITE Wait at least an hour before investigating a charge of dynamite that didn't go off.
Joe Kaiser, Covington, Kentucky

315. SHARPENING TOOLS RULE OF THREE
When you are sharpening a dull tool, stroke it across the sharpening stone for three times as long as you think you should. *Ned Bounds, sawyer, Salmon, Idaho*

316. SPLITTING KINDLING RULE OF TWO
When you think your kindling is split small enough, split it two more times. *Diane Gerhart, accountant*

317. HEATING A TRAVEL TRAILER To estimate the heater size for a travel trailer, figure 1000 BTUs per foot of length. A 15-foot trailer will need a 15,000-BTU heater. *Ralph Young, camper*

318. FLYING A SAILPLANE To determine the best speed to fly in wind, add half the wind speed to what you calculate otherwise.
John Campbell, glider pilot, Ann Arbor, Michigan

319. SELLING SUBSCRIPTIONS Increase the price of your magazine by 10 percent and you can expect to receive 10-percent fewer subscription orders.
Cathy Elton, circulation manager

320. CHOOSING A CROSS-COUNTRY SKI   You can size a cross-country ski by standing with one arm held straight in the air. A ski is the right length for you if it reaches from the floor to the palm of your hand.   *Donald Page, chemist*

321. MIXING FRESH ADOBE   Good adobe bricks are made from sandy clay or clay loam. If the mixture is too rich in clay, it will stick to your hoe; too rich in sand, your hoe will come up clean. The mixture is just right if it barely slips from your hoe, leaving traces of mud on the blade as you work it.
Marcia Southwick, writer and builder

322. BUILDING WALLS OF ADOBE   The height of an adobe wall should be less than ten times its thickness unless it is stiffened by buttresses or intersecting partitions.   *Marcia Southwick, writer and builder*

323. BUILDING A HOUSE OF ADOBE   The amateur builder should follow a few general rules: The total width of openings in a wall should not exceed 40 percent of its length; windows and doors should be at least 3 feet from corners; wall sections between windows and doors should be at least 3 feet long; and ceiling height should be 9 feet or less.
Marcia Southwick, writer and builder

To quickly figure the amp load of a light circuit use 1 amp per fixture or bulb.

324. DAIRY   The average dairy farm needs about three acres of land per cow for buildings, crops, and pasture.
William Menzi, cooperative extension agent

325. RUNNING A DAIRY   A good Holstein cow should produce about five gallons of milk a day for 305 days a year.   *Carol Gallagher, Lexington, Kentucky*

326. FEEDING A COW   One dairy cow eats one acre's worth of corn silage per year.
Monica Crispin, cooperative extension agent

327. RUNNING A DAIRY   A cow starts milking when it is two years old. It won't start making you any money until its second lactation, when it is three and a half years old.   *Chris Dahl, dairy farmer*

328. FEEDING DAIRY COWS For feeding dairy cows, three tons of corn silage equal one ton of hay.
Monica Crispin, cooperative extension agent

329. RUNNING A DAIRY You need half a ton of hay per cow per month, or six tons per cow per year.
Monica Crispin, cooperative extension agent

330. FEEDING A COW A cow should have three pounds of hay per day for every hundred pounds of weight.   *Roger Seeley, Albany, New York*

331. RAISING CORN You can expect to produce about eighteen tons of corn silage per acre per year.
George Shepard, farm help, Rochester, New York

332. RUNNING A DAIRY The average useful life of a dairy cow is five to seven years.
Chris Dahl, dairy farmer

333. EATING C-RATIONS If a can of C-rations has a B in the serial number, it probably contains fruit cocktail. *Dave Hinckle, Zolar Trucking*

334. PROGRAMMING A COMPUTER A computer program in a good high-level language can be written about five to ten times as fast as the same program in assembly language, but it will be longer and run slower. *Clifton Royston, programmer/analyst, Nukualofa, Tonga*

335. DESIGNING A COMPUTER SYSTEM When designing and coding a computer system, write as much of the system as possible in the highest level language available.
Clifton Royston, programmer/analyst, Nukualofa, Tonga

336. BUYING A DURABLE CAMERA If you want a durable camera, you should buy the simplest camera in the highest price range you can justify.
Robert B. Yepson, Jr., editor, The Durability Factor

337. CHECKING YOUR FIELDS FOR DRAINAGE Watch your fields as the snow melts in the spring. Poorly drained areas green up first.
Martin Stillwell, farmer

338. BUYING A LOCK The flatter the key, the more worthless the lock. *R. Siskind, baker*

339. JUNK MAIL You can figure that three out of four pieces of advertising mail are opened and glanced at. About one in four is opened and read thoroughly.
Carol Williams, Washington, D.C.

340. SOARING When flying a sailplane on a cross-country flight, fly toward the next thermal showing as much sink as you did lift in the previous thermal.
Dick Schreder, glider pilot

341. FLYING A SAILPLANE If you are above 3000 feet, stay on course. If you are between 2000 and 3000 feet, head for a good landing area. If you are between 1000 and 2000 feet, pick a landing field. If you are below 1000 feet, stick to the field you've picked. *Ed Byars, glider pilot*

342. RUNNING A RACE   Three times the average distance you run every day is close to the maximum distance you should run in a race.
Jeff Furman, business consultant

343. RUNNING A RACE   You won't have endurance for a race longer than one third of your average weekly training mileage.
Tom Werner, management consultant, Athens, Georgia

344. CHOOSING A SHOTGUN STOCK   You can quickly check the fit of a shotgun stock by holding it with your trigger arm. The butt of the stock should fit snuggly in the crotch of your elbow, with your hand on the grip and your finger on the trigger.
Wayne Jennings, maintenance mechanic, Cayutaville, New York

345. FINANCIAL SECURITY   For a minimum level of financial security, your net worth (the cash value of all of your assets) minus all your debts should equal one year's income.
J. Snyder, credit manager

346. FREE-LANCING RULE OF TWO   If you want a merely adequate return on a free-lance project like writing an article or a speech, figure out what you think you can get away with charging, and then double it. In 90 percent of the cases, you will get what you ask, and in 100 percent of the cases, the final expense and aggravation will exceed your original estimate by a considerable margin.
Joel Garreau, author

347. PRESERVING YOUR CAR   Diligently caring for your car with frequent washings, including the underbody, can add two years to its life.
Kenn Marash, writer

348. BUYING STOCK   For small investments, a stock needs to increase 10 percent in value just to break even after the broker's fees.
Christopher H. Stinson, CoEvolution Quarterly magazine

349. THROWING AWAY CLOTHING   Wait one year before throwing out a piece of clothing. If you haven't worn it in a year, you will never miss it.
Betsy Wackernagel, Ithaca, New York

350. RUNNING A RETAIL STORE Low-rent locations require more advertising. High-rent locations require less. For all locations, rent and advertising expenses combined should equal 10 percent of sales.
T. John Phillips, business consultant

351. ADDING STRAW TO ADOBE Straw is used as a binder to hold adobe bricks together as they dry. You can add up to a handful of very short pieces to a standard 4-by-10-by-14-inch brick. It will take slightly more than one large bale of straw to mix a thousand bricks. *Marcia Southwick, writer and builder*

352. STORING CORN Two bushels of ear corn equal one bushel of shell corn. *Martin Stilwell, farmer*

353. MAINTAINING AN AIR FORCE American, West German, and British air forces expect to have 40 percent of their aircraft under repair at any given time. *Brent Wiggins, artist and military buff*

354. PREDICTING RAIN If the barometric pressure is falling rapidly, a ring around the moon means rain in eighteen to twenty-four hours, about 75 percent of the time. *Paul E. Lehr, meteorologist*

355. LEADING INDICATORS Anytime the index of leading economic indicators moves in the same direction two months in a row, it means the economy will move that way in a few months.
Philip Greer, "When Do Indicators Stop Indicating?"

356. WRITING AN ADVERTISEMENT When writing an ad, use sentences of less than twelve words.
David Ogilvy, advertising expert, The Ogilvy and Mather Agency

357. USING A HOT TUB Soaking in a hot tub adds two to three pints of perspiration per hour per person to the water. *Phil Tomlinson, builder*

358. TESTING FREEZER TEMPERATURE A spoon will ring when rapped on a carton of ice cream if your freezer temperature is 0 degrees Fahrenheit or colder. *Cheryl Russell, demographer*

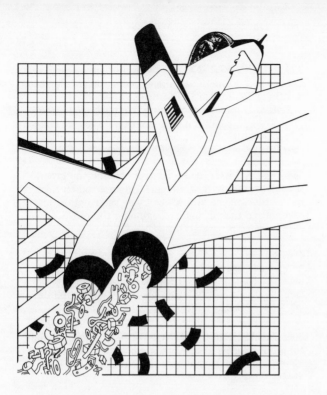

359. DEALING WITH DOUBT (WRITING) When in doubt, throw it out, along with gems, and jokes, and brilliant strokes.
Robert Lieberman, author, Paradise Rezoned

360. USING A MICROWAVE OVEN A simple test to determine if cookware is suitable for microwave is to set it in the oven empty; if it is hot to the touch after fifteen seconds of cooking, it should not be used.
The Joy of Cooking

361. HUMAN HORSEPOWER Working hard, the average person can generate about one-quarter horsepower. *Kevin Kelly, Athens, Georgia*

362. DESIGNING BILLBOARDS People are exposed to outdoor advertisements for only a few seconds. A good billboard should have no more than seven words and two things to look at.
Glen Lane, Massillon, Ohio

363. STUNT FLYING If the top of your head feels hot at the bottom of an outside loop, you should relax a little of the forward pressure on the control stick. Negative G forces are pushing too much blood into your brain, a condition that can cause a loss of consciousness, or "red out," if left unchecked.
Steve Poleskie, artist and stunt pilot

364. STUNT FLYING To avoid hitting the ground if your engine quits while performing a roll on take-off, accelerate the aircraft to twice the rotation speed of a normal takeoff before beginning the roll.
Steve Poleskie, artist and stunt pilot

365. STUNT FLYING Any tools missing in the hangar can usually be found in the tail of your plane near the control arms. These should be removed before flight, especially if you plan to do a roll on take-off. *Steve Poleskie, artist and stunt pilot*

366. MEASURING THINGS The first joint of your thumb measures about 1 inch, your foot measures about 1 foot, and your pace measures about 1 yard.
Stephen Gibian, architect and stonemason

367. FOLLOWING LOS ANGELES According to an authority at the University of California, the continental drift is such that Los Angeles is moving north toward San Francisco at about the rate your fingernails grow. *J. Eichelberger, Alameda, California*

368. LISTENING TO PEOPLE When someone speaks in a passive voice, he is trying to conceal something. *Alfred Kahn, economist*

369. BURNING SOLID FUELS When you are burning solid fuels, a 40-degree-Fahrenheit rise in stack temperature indicates a 1-percent reduction in combustion efficiency.
Scott Adams, central heating plant operator, Cornell University

370. GENERATING POWER When generating power on a large scale, no more than 15 percent should come from any one source. Things get screwed up when more than 15 percent of a system is out of service. *Joel Garreau, author*

371. WATCHING PEOPLE'S SHOULDERS Genuine emotion is always expressed with the entire body. When uncertain of a person's sincerity, watch their shoulders. You should doubt anyone who is speaking with strong emotion and relaxed shoulders.
D. Klein, painter, Brooklyn, New York

372. USING A TELEPHOTO LENS The longer the focal length of a lens, the more important it is to hold it steady, especially at slow shutter speeds. You can generally hand hold a camera with a shutter speed that is equal to the reciprocal of the focal length of the lens. Slower speeds require a tripod.
Jim Crissman, veterinary pathologist, Cornell University

373. FINDING DIRECTIONS Tall, pointed trees such as spruce usually have their tips leaning slightly to the north of east.
Alwyn T. Perrin, editor, Explorers Ltd. Source Book

374. WATCHING ANTS Food that ants like to eat is food that people should avoid (ants in our kitchen go for sweets and deep-fried tortilla chips).
David Leventer, psychotherapist, Santa Cruz, California

375. FINISHING A CABINET Finish work such as sanding, scraping, oiling, rubbing, and varnishing is 30 percent of any cabinetmaking job.
Dennis Pollack, cabinetmaker

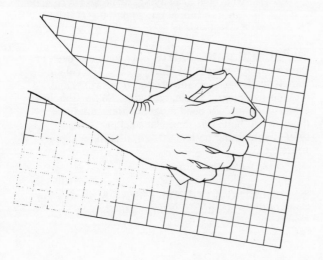

376. BRUSHING YOUR HAIR   Twenty-five brush strokes per day is considered optimal for best distribution of natural oils. More brushing causes damage.
Dr. Jonathan Zizmor, hair expert

377. FIXING YOUR HORSE'S BRIDLE   The cost of a good silver mounted spade bit is equal to one month's cowboy wages.
Douglass A. Pineo, biologist and falconer, Pullman, Washington

378. LEARNING A FOREIGN LANGUAGE   Half a semester of foreign language instruction at the college level is equal to one year of language instruction at the high school level.
David S. Russell, Minneapolis, Minnesota

379. AVOIDING THUNDERSTORMS WHILE FLYING   Clear the top of a known or suspected severe thunderstorm by at least 1000 feet of altitude for each ten knots of wind speed at the top of the cloud. This will exceed the altitude capability of most airplanes.
Airman's Information Manual

380. TALKING TO AN AMERICAN   If you are talking with an American whose legs are crossed and he wiggles his foot at what you say, he either disagrees with what you are saying, or he wants to add to it, or he wants to talk about something else.
The Blossoms, Fresno, California

381. PURCHASING PARTS   My boss has been in the research business for thirty years. His rule of thumb is: If you need something, buy two; chances are you will need it again, someday. So far, this has always paid off. I'll need a part of some kind and there it will be in our miscellaneous parts drawer, the twin of something he bought ten, fifteen, or twenty years ago.
Don Lewis, Folsom, Pennsylvania

382. SELLING A COUNTRY INN   A country inn should sell for about $20,000 per guest room.
Ellen Danke, quoting from the Wall Street Journal

383. BUILDING A PRISON   A new prison will cost about $100,000 per cell and take about three years to build.   *Louis Ganim, New York State Department of Corrections*

384. WIRING A HOUSE   To quickly estimate the amp load of a circuit, figure one amp per fixture or bulb.   *Ray Barbkenecht, counselor*

385. WEARING A WET SUIT   Scuba divers need a wet suit or some sort of protection against exposure when working in water that is colder than 75 degrees Fahrenheit.
Jack T. Marshall, professional diving instructor, Trumansburg, New York

386. TAKING A FEDERAL EXAM   On any government multiple-choice test, the longest answer is usually the correct one.   *Michael F. Brown, patent attorney*

387. PRUNING TREES   After pruning a tree, paint all wounds that are larger than your thumbnail.
Shelly Wade, tree specialist

388. SOUTH-FACING WINDOWS   One square foot of a south-facing window that is insulated at night will provide about 100,000 BTUs of heat per winter.
Robert Mendenhall, Boulder, Colorado

389. SAVING OIL RESOURCES   One square foot of a south-facing window that is insulated at night saves one gallon of oil per year.
Tom Wilson, energy consultant

390. DESIGNING A POTTERY KILN   For every foot of horizontal flue in a kiln, you need 2 extra feet of chimney to maintain a proper draft.
Daniel Rhodes, professor of ceramic art, Alfred University

391. WATCHING LEAVES   When trees start showing the whitish undersides of their leaves, it's getting ready to rain.
A. Bardsley, Mt. Kisco, New York

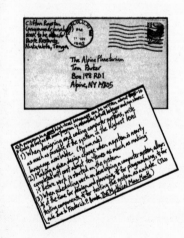

392. IDENTIFYING MINTS   All mints have square stems, but not all square stems are mints.
Scott M. Kruse, Yosemite National Park, California

393. SPORTS INJURIES   For pulled muscles, twisted joints, and other musculoskeletal injuries, use ice on new injuries, heat on old ones.
George Elliot, physical education teacher

394. DOUBLING YOUR MONEY   You can quickly calculate the number of years it will take to double your money by dividing the number seventy-two by your interest rate. For example, if your money is invested at 6-percent interest it will take seventy-two divided by six, or twelve, years to double.
Steve Parker, aerospace engineer, Princeton, New Jersey

395. DOUBLING YOUR POPULATION   You can quickly calculate the number of years it will take for a population to double by dividing the number seventy-two by the population's growth rate.
David T. Russell, high school teacher

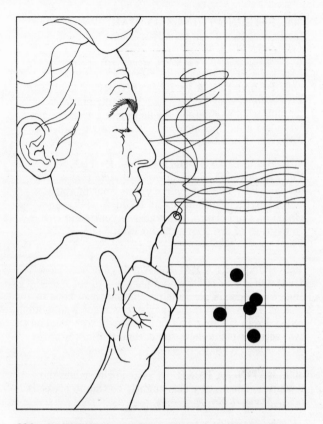

396. CARRYING A GUN If you can see the slightest part of the opening at the end of someone else's gun barrel, they are not handling their gun safely.
Peter F. Ayer, professor of music, West Bend, Wisconsin

397. SAILING IN HEAVY SEAS On a cruising sailboat in wind conditions that are increasing, canvas should be reduced the first time it seems like a good idea. *Michael Spencer, lawyer, San Francisco, California*

398. MAKING A DECISION There are three valid answers to a yes or no question: yes, no, and no decision right now. Eighty percent of all bad decisions are snap decisions. Good managers make the best decisions after "sleeping on it." *Joseph Stein, business consultant, Arcata, California*

399. SELLING THINGS BY MAIL   Inexpensive mail-order items will usually sell best at round dollar prices ($2, $3, $5).
L. Perry Wilbur, mail-order expert, Money in Your Mailbox

400. PLANNING A PUBLIC-ADDRESS SYSTEM Professional sound crews plan on using one watt of amplification per person for an indoor audience, a watt and a half per person for an outdoor audience.
James Arthur, sound engineer

401. MEASURING SOMETHING IN THE SKY You can describe the location of objects that are low in the sky by holding your hand in front of you at arm's length. With your palm facing in and your pinkie on the horizon, the width of your hand covers 15 degrees of arc above the horizon.
Hugh Crowell, Columbus, Ohio

402. RUNNING A RACE   Watch your pace closely for the first half of a race and try not to cut more than five seconds per mile off the pace you hope to run. Every second more than five you cut from your mile pace in the first half of a race will cost you one to two seconds per mile in the second half of the race.
Jim Crissman, veterinary pathologist, Cornell University

403. EATING A PEAR   A pear is ripe when the flesh near the stem yields slightly to thumb pressure.
Gladys Sherwood, Memphis, Tennessee

404. DRINKING LIQUOR   As far as getting drunk is concerned, one jigger of liquor is equal to a twelve-ounce beer.   *Robert Morley, unemployed*

405. DRINKING AND DRIVING   If you are going to drive home from a party, don't have more than one drink per hour.   *Betsy Green, painter*

406. MANAGING SUBORDINATES   Most managers can effectively handle eight or nine subordinates.
SMC Hendrick, Inc., management consultants, Framingham, Massachusetts

407. FREE-LANCING   Free-lance artists and designers should expect to put in one unbillable hour for every billable hour.   *Mike Rider, art director*

TOM PARKER
BOX 198, RD 1
ALPINE, N.Y.
14805

Magazine publishers' rule of thumb: Increase the price by 10 percent, and you can expect to receive 10 percent fewer subscription orders.
Cathy Etter
Circulation Manager

408. TAKING FISH FROM YOUR POND   Bluegills will overrun your bass if you don't keep the population in balance. Take out fifteen times as many bluegills as bass. By weight, take out two or three pounds of bluegill for every pound of bass.
Cornell University

409. PLANNING A HIGHWAY   A divided highway will occupy about forty acres of land per mile. Other roads occupy between six and twelve acres per mile.
William S. Stevens, highway engineer

410. USING A BRICK BAKE OVEN   There are some traditional methods to tell when an oven is ready to use: (1) The bricks must all look red. If the black spots are not all burned off, it is not hot enough. (2) Sprinkle flour on the oven hearth; if it burns black right away, the oven is too hot. (3) Insert the tender part of your wrist toward the inner corners of the oven behind the front walls and count. If you cannot hold your hand in longer than to count to twenty, it is hot enough. If you can count to thirty, it is not hot enough for bread.
Richard Bacon, writer and historian

411. USING A MICROWAVE OVEN   With your microwave oven at its most powerful setting, figure one and a half to two minutes per cup of casserole.
Irma Dalton, artist, Westminster, California

412. CALORIES AND BACKPACKING   A 165-pound backpacker will need about 4500 calories per day under normal conditions and somewhat more in winter. Fats should provide about 20 percent of your calorie intake, protein about 5 percent, and carbohydrates the rest.
Alwyn Perrin, Explorers Ltd. Source Book

413. THE SALES RULE OF 80-20   Salespeople should talk only 20 percent of the time during their first visit with a potential customer and listen the other 80 percent. During later visits, the salespeople should do most of the talking to sell the benefits of their products.
Andrew Keaton, national sales manager, The Dietzgen Corporation

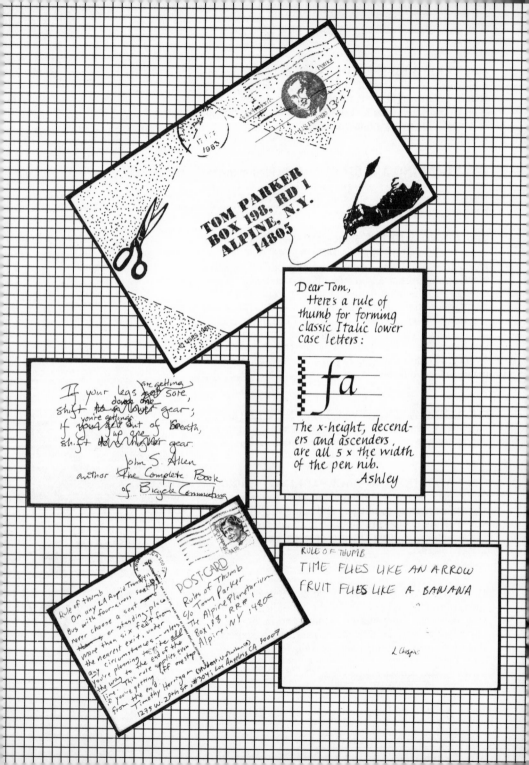

TOM PARKER
BOX 198, RD 1
ALPINE, N.Y.
14805

Dear Tom,
 Here's a rule of
thumb for forming
classic Italic lower
case letters:

fa

The x-height, decend-
ers and ascenders,
are all 5 x the width
of the pen nib.
 Ashley

If your legs are getting sore,
shift to a lower gear;
if you're getting out of breath,
shift up one gear.
 John S. Allen
author The Complete Book
 of Bicycle Commuting

Rule of thumb
On any LA Rapid Transit
Bus with four-across seating
never choose a seat or standing place
more than six feet from
the nearest exit, under
any circumstances—unless
you're planning to ride all
the way to the end of the
line. This rule applies even
if you're getting off one stop
from Timothy Herrigan (student, urbanologist)
1275 W. 29th St. #204, Los Angeles CA 90007

POSTCARD
Rules of Thumb
Tom Parker
c/o Alpine Planetarium
The Alpine Planetarium
Box 198, RR#1
Alpine, NY 14805

RULE OF THUMB
TIME FLIES LIKE AN ARROW
FRUIT FLIES LIKE A BANANA

L. Chisgis

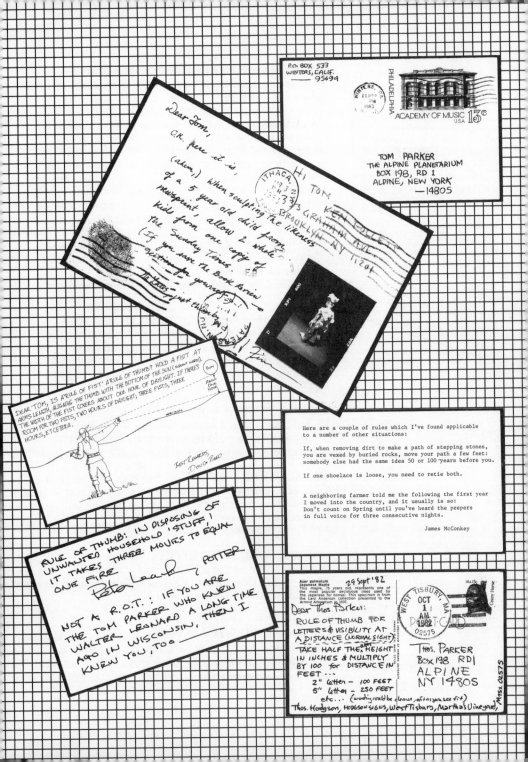

Postcard (top right):

P.O. BOX 533
WINTERS, CALIF.
— 95694

PHILADELPHIA
ACADEMY OF MUSIC
USA 13¢

WINTERS, CA
FEB 2 PM 1983

TOM PARKER
THE ALPINE PLANETARIUM
BOX 198, RD 1
ALPINE, NEW YORK
— 14805

Postcard (upper left):

Dear Tom,

O.K. here it is,

(ahem,) When sculpting the likeness
of a 5 year old child from
newsprint, allow 2 whole
kids from the Sunday Times.
(If you save the Book Review
section for yourself—
the Arts—just taken by J.)

HI TOM
KEN GRAHAM AVE
BROOKLYN, NY 11201

ITHACA
1983

PARKER

Postcard (middle left, fisherman illustration):

DEAR TOM, IS A 'RULE OF FIST' A 'RULE OF THUMB'? HOLD A FIST AT
ARM'S LENGTH, ALIGNING THE THUMB WITH THE BOTTOM OF THE SUN (SQUINT HARD!).
THE WIDTH OF THE FIST COVERS ABOUT ONE HOUR OF DAYLIGHT; IF THERE'S
ROOM FOR TWO FISTS, TWO HOURS OF DAYLIGHT; THREE FISTS, THREE
HOURS, ETCETERA.

SUN
ABOUT ONE
HOUR

HORIZON

BEST REGARDS,
DOUG PINEO

Letter (lower left):

RULE OF THUMB: IN DISPOSING OF
UNWANTED HOUSEHOLD 'STUFF,'
IT TAKES THREE MOVES TO EQUAL
ONE FIRE.

POTTER

Peter Leach,

NOT A R.O.T.: IF YOU ARE
THE TOM PARKER WHO KNEW
WALTER LEONARD A LONG TIME
AGO IN WISCONSIN, THEN I
KNEW YOU, TOO —

Typed note (center right):

Here are a couple of rules which I've found applicable
to a number of other situations:

If, when removing dirt to make a path of stepping stones,
you are vexed by buried rocks, move your path a few feet:
somebody else had the same idea 50 or 100 years before you.

If one shoelace is loose, you need to retie both.

A neighboring farmer told me the following the first year
I moved into the country, and it usually is so:
Don't count on Spring until you've heard the peepers
in full voice for three consecutive nights.

James McConkey

Postcard (lower right, Japanese Maple):

Acer palmatum
Japanese Maple
This maple, 75 years old, represents one of
the most popular deciduous trees used by
the Japanese for bonsai. This specimen is from
the Larz Anderson collection presented to the
Arnold Arboretum in 1937.

29 Sept '82

WEST TISBURY, MA
OCT 1 AM 1982
02575

USA 13¢
Crazy Horse

POST-CARD

Dear Thos. Parker:
RULE OF THUMB FOR
LETTERS & VISIBILITY AT
A DISTANCE (NORMAL SIGHT):
TAKE HALF THE HEIGHT
IN INCHES & MULTIPLY
BY 100 for DISTANCE IN
FEET —
2" letter — 100 FEET
5" letter — 250 FEET
etc... (wording could be cleaner, alter as you see fit)

Thos. Hodgson, HODGSON SIGNS, West Tisbury, Martha's Vineyard,

Thos. PARKER
Box 198 RD1
ALPINE
NY 14805

Mass. 02575

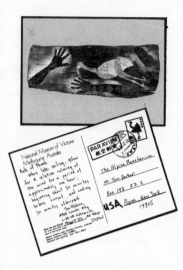

414. PAVING WITH BRICKS A crew of six brick-layers with one foreman can lay 1000 square feet of paving brick per day. *R. Pieper, architectural historian*

415. PASSING A CAR If you are passing another car on a two-lane road and are confronted with a car coming toward you, there are two things you can do: accelerate or brake. You should brake; in all cars the brakes are a lot more powerful than the engine. The only time you shouldn't brake is if another car is right behind you also passing. In that case, your luck has run out anyway. *J. Baldwin, designer and writer*

416. OFFENDING PEOPLE The people who offend others most easily are often the most easily offended themselves.
Joel R. Stegall, dean, Ithaca College School of Music, Ithaca, New York

417. HOSTING A PARTY Do not invite a deter-mined raconteur to a party to be held in a space of less than 600 square feet, not counting the piano. Otherwise, it will be hard for people to escape him or her, as the case may be, without walking out on you. *John Boyd, florist*

418. PLANNING A POND In most of the eastern United States, you'll need a five-acre watershed to supply a one-acre pond fed entirely by run-off water. *G. Hickey, heavy equipment operator*

419. SELLING A RETAIL BUSINESS If you can't think of a reasonable price to sell a retail business, a good starting point is one year's gross income; but you probably will have to settle for less. *John Pitkin, photographer*

420. WORKING WITH RIVETS Before it is hammered, the end of a rivet should stick out slightly more than its own diameter. This will give you enough metal to form a solid head. *Mike Bauer, sheet metal worker*

421. WORKING WITH RIVETS Install a rivet at least one and a half times its diameter from the edge of the piece it is in. *Mike Bauer, sheet metal worker*

422. WORKING WITH RIVETS You can figure that a properly riveted joint will have three fourths of the strength of the pieces it joins together.
Mike Bauer, sheet metal worker

423. PREDICTING A FROST When the temperature falls below 50 degrees Fahrenheit at sunset, watch out for morning frost.
Tim Matson, Thetford Center, Vermont

424. WAITING FOR GOOD WEATHER The rain is over when dry spots appear on the blacktop.
Dorinda Ryan, Manuchula, Florida

425. UNTANGLING SOMETHING To untangle anything stringlike keep pulling the mess outward, making it larger and looser until the loops untangle themselves. This is your only hope of success.
Kevin Kelly, Athens, Georgia

426. UNTANGLING YOURSELF If you are lost in the woods, always travel downstream. If you are lost in the astral plane, always travel toward the light.
Pat Morningstar, anthropologist, Tallahassee, Florida

427. UPHOLSTERING A SOFA It takes between 10 and 12 yards of fabric to reupholster a full-size sofa.
Phil Tomlinson, builder

428. THE SIZE OF YOUR HEAD Your body is eight times the height of your head, your shoulders are twice the width of your head, and your foot is equal to the height of your head.
Scott Parker, Beaumont, Texas

429. EATING MEALS Most people eat their largest meal at supper, when their bodies need it least. As a rule, you should eat breakfast like a king, lunch like a prince, and supper like a pauper.
Jane Brody, nutrition columnist, The New York Times

430. HUNTING FOR DEER The vital area on a whitetail deer is about the size of a paper plate. Never shoot from farther away than you can consistently hit a paper plate.
Dr. Timothy Haywood, physicist, Wilmington, North Carolina

431. KNEADING BREAD Knead bread for eight minutes. If you knead it more, it will have too much air.

Leslie Warren, music teacher, Kittery Point, Maine

432. LYNN FELLOWS' PENCIL TEST Before throwing a pot on a potter's wheel, test your clay for plasticity. Wrap a pencil-sized stick of clay around your index finger. If the sample breaks or cracks in a number of places, it will not throw well.

Lynn Fellows, potter

433. ANN LANDERS' PENCIL TEST To determine whether you need to wear a bra, place a pencil under your breast. If the pencil falls to the floor, you don't need to wear a bra; if it stays, you need one.

Ann Landers, advice columnist

434. OPENING A BOTTLE OF WINE When deciding when to open a bottle of wine, remember most wine is as good when it's a year old as it will ever be and will go downhill after its third birthday.

The Joy of Cooking

435. PUTTING OUT A FIRE Direct your fire extinguisher at the base of the flames from a distance of less than 10 feet. If you can't get any closer than 10 feet, the fire is probably too large for a hand-held fire extinguisher. Concentrate your efforts on leaving the vicinity of the fire.

Norman Lewis, volunteer fireman

436. STORING HEAT IN A GREENHOUSE
Containers of water are excellent for storing heat in a solar greenhouse. Start with 1 cubic foot of water for each square foot of greenhouse glass.

Janet Hopper, New York City

437. WAKING UP IN CALIFORNIA When you wake up on a California winter morning and the stars outside your window shine without twinkling, put on your long underwear.

Rob Weinberg, Tassajara Zen Mountain Center, Carmel Valley, California

438. FOLLOWING A COLD FRONT You can expect a well-developed cold front to travel at more than thirty miles per hour, especially in winter and spring when cold fronts tend to be fastest.
Stephen Friends, meteorologist

439. BEGINNING WITH BEES Getting started with honeybees will cost you $100 per hive with bees and equipment.   *Larry Meyer, beekeeper*

440. STARTING A DAIRY Getting started in the dairy business will cost you $5000 per cow in animals, land, buildings, and equipment.
William Menzi, cooperative extension agent

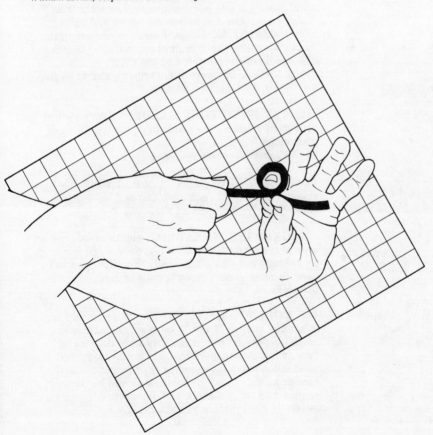

441. BUILDING A HOUSE It takes four experienced builders about four hundred hours to build an average-sized house.
Thomas Peterson, builder

442. CATCHING FISH Wind from the west, fishing is best; wind from the east, fishing is least.
J. J. Everhart, retired, Spartanburg, South Carolina

443. CATCHING FISH A wind from the south blows a hook in the mouth. In the fall of the year when a lake has cooled off there will often be a warm sunny day with a slight southerly wind. On these occasions the sun heats the top layer of water, and the wind pushes it into northern bays. The warmth of the water causes the fish to become active and can set off a sudden feeding binge. Reservoir anglers in the South sometimes encounter these warming trends in the middle of the winter, and the smart ones are ready to move to where the warmer water is located.
Chet Meyers and Al Lindner, fishing experts

444. WATERING YOUR GARDEN Don't water your garden unless the soil is dry past the depth of your index finger.
Caroline Eckstrom, managing editor

445. MEETING WOMEN Under ideal circumstances, a man will seek a woman half his age plus seven years. *Elaine Renner, Ithaca, New York*

446. GROWING WHEAT One eighth of an acre, an area about 50 by 100 feet, will grow enough wheat for an average homesteading family. For this, you will need to plant about fifteen pounds of seed.
Richard Bacon, writer and historian

447. COLUMNS OF TYPE The more quickly a column of type is meant to be read, the narrower it should be. Books can have fairly wide columns of type, while newspapers that are quickly skimmed need much narrower columns. For magazines and similar publications, the columns should be the width required to set one and a half alphabets of lower-case letters in the typeface you are using.
Ray Bruman, Berkeley, California

448. CRACKING NUTS   A pound of nuts in the shell yields about half a pound shelled.
The Joy of Cooking

449. PLAYING IT SAFE   Never play poker with anyone called Doc. Never eat at a restaurant called Mom's.   *Anonymous*

450. USING YOUR MONEY   A dollar bill is about 6 inches long.
Jeffrey Bald, piano tuner and guitar maker, San Jose, California

451. JUMPING ABILITY   The distance from the heel to the articulation of the calf muscle is an indication of jumping ability. For high-jumping dancers and athletes, the distance should be equal to or greater than the length of the foot.
Stephanie Judy, writer, British Columbia, Canada

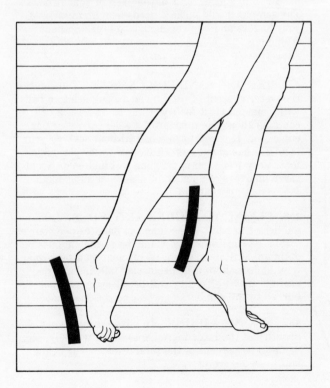

452. INVITING GUESTS If you are giving a party and you live in the suburbs, invite two times the number of people you want to attend. If you live within range of public transportation, invite one and a half times the number of people you want. If you are in the heart of the city, invite one and a quarter times the number of people you want.
Janet Blum, Denver, Colorado

453. TESTING THE TEXTURE OF DIRT You can decide whether to disc harrow a field or not by balling up some dirt, holding it with both hands at arm's length, and dropping it. If the dirtball doesn't break, it is too wet to disc. *Peter van Berkum, Kittery Point, Maine*

454. TESTING FOUNDRY SAND You can test a sample of foundry sand for casting by scooping up a handful and squeezing it in the palm of your hand. The sample should make a good clean impression of your fingers and be firm enough to break without crumbling.
Howard Spencer, Elmira, New York

455. TESTING SAND FOR CEMENT You can test the water content of sand by squeezing it into a ball with your fist. If it feels wet but won't form a ball, it contains about one quarter of a gallon of water per cubic foot. If it will form a ball without soaking your hands, it has about half a gallon of water per cubic foot. Very wet sand is dripping wet and holds about three quarters of a gallon of water per cubic foot.
Bob Syvanen, concrete expert

456. FLYING TO HIGHER ALTITUDES It is inefficient to climb more than ten minutes per hour of estimated time en route. Climbing to the engine's optimum altitude may not be efficient on a particular trip. Unless there are spectacular tailwinds, high-altitude cruise efficiency will be offset by the fuel burned in the climb. *Bruce Landsberg, pilot and writer*

457. MIXING A DRINK In mixed drinks, keep the quantity of the basic ingredient — gin, whiskey, etc. — up to 60 percent of the total drink, never below half. *The Joy of Cooking*

CORTINOVIS
1130 ORCHARD RD.
LAFAYETTE, CA. 94549
DAN CORTINOVIS
SANITARY ENGINEER

TOM PARKER
BOX 198, RD 1
ALPINE, N.Y.
14805

THE AVERAGE HUMAN PRODUCES 0.2 POUNDS PER DAY (DRY WEIGHT) OF BODY WASTES. ANAEROBIC DIGESTION OF THIS MATERIAL PRODUCES 18 CUBIC FT OF GAS PER POUND OF SOLIDS DESTROYED. THE HEAT VALUE IS 650 BTU/CUBIC FOOT. OF GAS

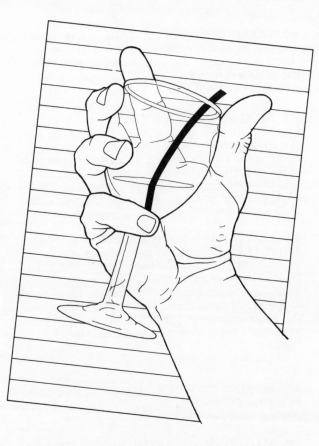

458. FISHING FOR TROUT If you can see the fish; the fish can see you. *Grant Wootton, fly-fishing pundit*

459. LOGGING Sapling conifers will lean away from a larger tree and/or in the direction of the prevailing breezes. *Ned Bounds, sawyer, Salmon, Idaho*

460. CALLING FOR HELP If you are assaulted, scream Fire! People are more likely to come to your aid than if you shout Help! *Boardroom Reports*

461. FISHING TROUT The first cast is critical; your chances of catching a fish diminish with each cast. *Sheridan Anderson, author, The Curtis Creek Manifesto*

462. SELLING THINGS BY MAIL Using direct mail ads, or what is commonly called "junk mail," it is almost impossible to make money selling something that costs less than $10.

J. Persiponco, Centerville, Indiana

463. MAXIMIZING YOUR RANGE IN AN AIR-PLANE You will get your maximum range by flying at a speed that equals the airplane's "best-rate-of-climb" speed plus 25 percent. This speed will be close to the 45 percent power setting that is usually the lowest shown on range charts or graphs. In some aircraft, you may only gain a few miles, but they could make a difference. *Bruce Landsberg, pilot and writer*

464. MAXIMIZING YOUR ENDURANCE IN AN AIRPLANE Maximum endurance in an airplane is attained at its "best-rate-of-climb" speed, or Vy. Vy, listed in the airplane's manual, approximates the maximum lift-over-drag ratio; it requires the least amount of power to maintain level flight. If you become lost, this speed will stretch the fuel supply and give you more time to spot landmarks or summon help by radio.

Bruce Landsberg, pilot and writer

465. MAKING CLOTHES Always sew the seams on a garment from the hem up.

Madeleine Yardley, art teacher, Worcester, Massachusetts

466. MAGAZINE ADVERTISEMENTS The average woman reads four ads in an average issue of an average magazine.

David Ogilvy, advertising expert. The Ogilvy and Mather Agency

467. WRITING ADVERTISEMENTS A good ad will have at least fourteen references to people for every one hundred words of copy.

David Ogilvy, advertising expert, The Ogilvy and Mather Agency

468. FUR TRAPPING You can tell the condition of an animal pelt by looking at the fleshy side. Pelts that are blue when skinned or turn blue as they dry on a stretcher have not reached their prime.

J. E. Wertenbach, trapper

469. POLITICAL ELECTIONS   The better
the weather on election day, the better it is for
Democrats.   *Mike Rider, art director*

470. HOW MUCH TO WIN AT POKER   It is time
to quit for the day if you have doubled your money.
However, if the cards are still going your way, rein-
vest 20 percent of your till. If you lose that, leave the
game at once.   *Edwin Silverstang, games expert*

471. WRITING COMPUTER SOFTWARE   A software writer can be expected to generate about ten
lines of debugged, high-order language a day.
Anonymous systems engineer

472. PLANTING TOMATOES   When set in the
field, a young tomato plant should be as wide as it is
high. Taller plants are leggy and more prone to wind
damage.   *Peter van Berkum, Kittery Point, Maine*

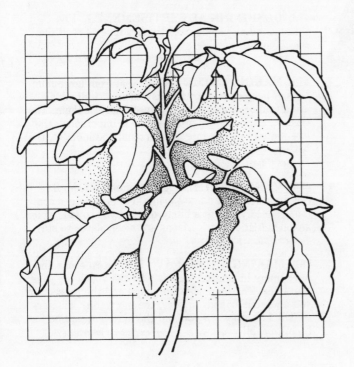

473. LISTENING TO TRAINS Loud train, plan on rain. *Lewis Ramsey, historical restorations contractor*

474. MEASURING THINGS A pint's a pound, the world around.
Jeffrey Bald, San Jose, California, and countless other people

475. GETTING A JOB Most job seekers can expect one to four job leads and/or interviews for every forty telephone calls they make.
Karen E. O'Neill, career consultant, Englewood, Colorado

476. WATCHING A BOXING MATCH A boxer has delivered an effective blow to the body if his opponent lifts one foot clear of the ground.
Angelo Dundee, boxing authority

477. REBUILDING AN ENGINE You can plan on a complete automobile engine overhaul costing $2 to $3 per cubic inch of cylinder displacement.
LeRoi Smith, writer and car builder

478. DESIGNING ADVERTISEMENTS Five times as many people read the headline as read the rest of an ad.
David Ogilvy, advertising expert, The Ogilvy and Mather Agency

479. MAKING CRIME PAY Steal from large numbers of people as indirectly as possible. Individuals are afraid of crimes directed specifically at them. The threat disappears when the crime is impersonal, the loss indirect — the more impersonal and indirect, the better.
Stephen Gillers, journalist

480. MAKING CRIME PAY Commit a federal crime rather than a state crime. Federal judges are more worldly and less likely to send you to jail, or for as long. Also federal prisons are nicer places to stay.
Stephen Gillers, journalist

481. MAKING CRIME PAY Look prosperous and have many influential friends who can vouch for your character. The more like the judge and the prosecutor you and your friends appear, the more they will personally identify with you and the harder it will be for them to send you away. *Stephen Gillers, journalist*

482. MAKING CRIME PAY Commit a crime that a judge can relate to. *Stephen Gillers, journalist*

483. MAKING CRIME PAY Before committing a crime, study the sentencing statistics in your jurisdiction. If you get caught in a state where a tough judge will throw the book at you, you have only yourself and your poor preparation to blame.
Stephen Gillers, journalist

484. MAKING CRIME PAY If you get caught, have someone higher to turn to. If you can give the prosecutor a "bigger" fish, you will get a lesser sentence or possibly not be prosecuted at all.
Stephen Gillers, journalist

485. PASSING A KIDNEY STONE A urinary calculus, or kidney stone, that is less than 10 millimeters in diameter will generally pass out of the body on its own. *James Macmillan, M.D.*

486. PREDICTING SNOW You should expect deep snow when hornets build their nests higher than usual.
Robert B. Thomas, The Old Farmer's Almanac

487. ADJUSTING BICYCLE HANDLEBARS The distance from the front of your seat to the handlebar cross member should equal the length of your forearm from elbow to fingertip.
Peter van Berkum, Kittery Point, Maine

488. PLANNING A HIKE To estimate your hiking time, figure half an hour for each mile plus half an hour for each 1000-foot increase in altitude.
Pierre Gremaud, Waitsfield, Vermont

489. PLANNING A HIKE To estimate your hiking time, figure one hour for every three miles plus one hour for every 2000-foot increase in elevation.
Kevin Kelly, Athens, Georgia

490. FORECASTING THE WEATHER When first-graders get disruptive as a class, there's going to be a major change in weather.
Lin Spaeth, first grade teacher

491. THE SURVIVAL RULE OF THREE You can live three seconds without blood, three minutes without air, three days without water, and three weeks without food.
Sandy Figuers, geologist, El Paso, Texas

492. THE SECOND SURVIVAL RULE OF THREE History shows that people repeatedly survive far longer than thought possible. A general rule is to estimate the survival time for a particular person under specific conditions, then multiply by three.
Tim J. Setnicka, author, Wilderness Search and Rescue

493. ADJUSTING YOUR CAR SEAT You should check your seat adjustment with your hands at the ten and two o'clock positions on the steering wheel. You should be close enough so that you can make almost a full half-turn of the wheel without having to lean forward or having your elbows touch your body.
Alan Johnson, SCCA national driving champion

494. LANDING AN AIRPLANE Begin your descent five miles out for every 1000 feet of altitude you have to lose. If you are 8000 feet above the ground, start your descent forty miles from the airport.
Bruce Landsberg, pilot and writer

495. TAPPING MAPLE TREES FOR SAP Wind north to west, the flow is best; wind south to east, the flow is least. *Karen Spaulding, Concord, New Hampshire*

496. TRAPPING LOBSTERS Plan on losing about 33 percent of your lobster pots each year to storms and heavy seas.
T. M. Prudden, lobster expert

497. CALORIES AND RESTING The average person, resting comfortably for twenty-four hours, will burn about 1700 calories.
Steve Hinshaw, Farmland, Indiana

498. STARTING A BUSINESS Anyone starting a small business should have a bankroll that is twice the sum of every conceivable expense.
Jeff Furman, business consultant

499. BLUFFING AT POKER Don't bluff during
the first hour of play or when your strong hands are
being called. A good time to bluff is after you have
won two or three pots in a row.
Dale Armstrong, card player

500. AIMING YOUR ADVERTISEMENTS To
attract women, show babies and women. To attract
men, show men.
David Ogilvy, advertising expert, The Ogilvy and Mather Agency

501. FEEDING PEOPLE For long trips and expe-
ditions, plan on taking at least two pounds of food per
person per day. *G. Brooks, Flagstaff, Arizona*

502. DROPPING ANCHOR Under normal conditions use 7 feet of anchor line for each foot of water.
If the water is 10 feet deep, you'll need 70 feet of
anchor line. *Peter Kim, San Diego, California*

503. SHOOTING FILM A professional photographer feels pleased if he or she gets one good shot on a
roll of film. *Jeff Furman, business consultant*

504. DRIVING A RACE CAR If a track is new to you, always use a higher gear than you think you're going to need in a turn. This will help prevent you from overrevving on a corner that surprises you and may keep you from doing something embarrassing.
Alan Johnson, SCCA national driving champion

505. CARING FOR NEW WOODWORK Rub linseed oil into new woodwork once a day for a week, once a week for a month, once a month for a year, and once a year from then on.
Marilyn Rider, school administrator

506. SERVING DRINKS When you are planning drinks for a party, figure two drinks per guest for the first half hour and one drink per hour after that.
Lisa Dahl, conference manager, Aurora, New York

507. BREAKING IN A NEW CHAINSAW When breaking in a new chainsaw, adjust the chain tension twice during the first tank of fuel, once during the second tank, and once every other tank for the rest of the day.
Ned Bounds, sawyer, Salmon, Idaho

508. JOGGING Jogging is difficult and painful the first six weeks, hard work for the next six weeks, and as easy as walking from then on.
Dr. Larry R. Hunt, Toronto, Ontario

509. FINDING CAVES In the colder parts of the country, you will often find caves in areas where the soil is red.
David R. McClurg, speleologist

510. USING LIGHTS If you have to leave a room for more than a minute, turn off the lights. Otherwise, leave them on. For fluorescent lights, use one hour as the rule.
Bob Horton, statistics consultant, West Lafayette, Indiana

511. CALLING A BET In a poker game, call a bet when you have better than two out of five chances of winning the pot and do not risk more than you stand to gain if you do win.
Professor Horace C. Levinson, mathematician

Rule of Thumb:

you may see a rainbow to the east or west of you, never to the north or south.

Rhiannon

RHIANNON
3000 Center St #100
Berkeley, CA 94704

Rules of Thumb
The Alpine Planetarium
Box 198 RD 1
Alpine, NY 14805

512. DEALING WITH DOUBT (MOTORCYCLE RACING) When in doubt, gas it.
Anonymous motorcycle racer

513. TEACHING To teach effectively, a teacher should limit a class to twenty-five students. A class of twenty-five to thirty-two students should have a teacher's aide. A group with more than thirty-two students should be split into two classes.
Leslie Warren, music teacher, Kittery Point, Maine

514. TEACHING For student-paced teaching you need one teacher for every ten students. For teacher-paced teaching, one teacher for every thirty students will do.
Tom Werner, management consultant, Athens, Georgia

515. RAISING FISH IN SILOS Catfish can be raised for food inside a solar greenhouse. They are kept in translucent silos filled with water. If at their first daily feeding the catfish rapidly swim to the surface, stick their heads out of the water, and gulp for food, everything is O.K. If they are sluggish or don't come to the surface, promptly change the water.
John Todd, The New Alchemy Institute, Woods Hole, Massachusetts

516. STORING WATER A bomb shelter needs a gallon of water per day per person for drinking and washing. *D. Riley, maintenance crew supervisor*

517. SELLING APPLIANCES When greeting a customer, make sure your first remark refers directly to the product you hope to sell.
Mike Hart, appliance dealer

518. TAKING PICTURES UNDER WATER Most leaks in an underwater camera housing show up at very shallow depths. If no leaks appear within 15 feet of the surface, there is a 95-percent chance that none will appear at greater depths.
Flip Schulke, underwater photographer

519 TAKING A PICTURE A good guide for exposing film on a clear day with the sun at your back is to set the aperture at f16 and the shutter speed to the ASA of the film. *Jon Reis, photographer*

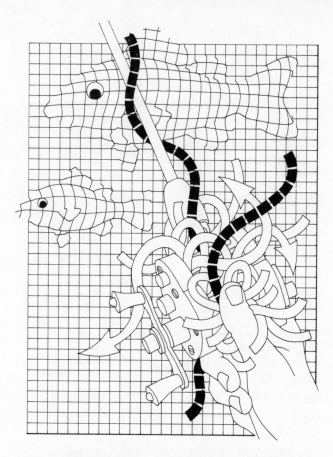

520. FISHING FOR TROUT If you don't catch anything after seven casts, move on to the next likely spot on the stream. Three casts should be enough for pockets and holes that are less than 8 feet in diameter. *Sheridan Anderson, author, The Curtis Creek Manifesto*

521. MAKING A TV COMMERCIAL Limit yourself to one sales point per television commercial.
Jennifer Johnson, Knoxville, Tennessee

522. GIVING A SPEECH You should expect the actual speech to take one-third more time than it took you during practice.
Bert Decker, Decker Communications, San Francisco, California

523. LECTURING IN BULGARIA If you are speaking English to Bulgarians, write twenty minutes of material for a sixty-minute speech to allow time for translation. *Robert Horvitz, artist*

524. SELLING A PAINTING Paintings in galleries sell for twice the price they sell for at art auctions. *Richard Merkin, painter*

525. MAKING A MOVIE Movie credits and sub-titles should appear on the screen long enough to be read three times. *Jim Maas, film maker*

526. RAISING MONEY University fund raisers plan on getting one-third of their money from ten big contributors, one-third from one hundred medium contributors, and one-third from everyone else. *Anonymous university fund raiser*

527. CHECKING A ROPE Plan on using a rope for only two or three caving seasons, then retire it from critical use. *David R. McClurg, speleologist*

528. CHECKING A ROPE A caving rope should be retired after one hundred days of use. *The British Mountaineering Council*

529. CHECKING A ROPE Get a new rope when 50 percent of the surface strands are worn to fuzz. *Peggy Kerber, editor, Mountaineering*

530. CHECKING A ROPE A climbing rope is over-due for retirement when you can no longer feel the separate strands as your hand slides along it. *Peggy Kerber, editor, Mountaineering*

531. BUYING A HAT Your wedding ring size is the same as your hat size. *Doris Jennings, printer's assistant*

532. SAILING A CANOE On an extended voyage along the coast of Alaska and British Columbia, three quarters of your time will be spent paddling, but half your distance will be covered in the one quarter of the time spent under sail. *George B. Dyson, boatbuilder, British Columbia, Canada*

533. FOLLOWING ANOTHER CAR You should keep at least one car length between your car and the car ahead for every ten miles per hour of speed.
Carla Corin, biologist, Eagle River, Alaska

534. HELPING BEES THROUGH THE WINTER It is important to leave enough honey in a hive to feed your bees through the winter. One rule is leave ten pounds of honey for each month that winter lasts in your area.
Larry Meyer, beekeeper

535. RISING AIR Rising air cools about 5.5 degrees Fahrenheit per 1000 feet. Sinking air warms at the same rate.
Stephen Friends, meteorologist

536. CALM AIR Calm air is also cooler with altitude — about 3.5 degrees Fahrenheit per 1000 feet.
Scott M. Kruse, Yosemite National Park, California

537. WILDERNESS TRAVEL For best speed in unmarked wilderness, always aim for the heaviest timber.
Peggy Kerber, editor, Mountaineering

538. PACKING WITH HORSES You need at least three variations of each meal for pack trips lasting more than a week. Anything less gets monotonous.
Francis Davis Long Eddy, packer

539. THE TRAVELING RULE OF TWO When traveling, take twice the money and half the clothes you think you will need.
Betsy Wackernagel, Ithaca, New York

540. SHOPPING FOR FRESHNESS In a well-run retail store, the freshest items come from the back of the shelf. *Truman Plant, expressman*

541. GROWING HOTHOUSE TOMATOES It takes about $2000 to heat a standard-size, 28-by-96-foot double-wall greenhouse through spring tomato season in New Hampshire.
Peter van Berkum, Kittery Point, Maine

542. PLAYING SCRABBLE As a rule, I can beat anyone at scrabble who does crossword puzzles better than I. *Sharon Yntema, author, Vegetarian Baby*

543. COOKING SPAGHETTI Your thumb and index finger will encircle four modest servings of uncooked spaghetti. *James Colby, civil engineer*

544. DEBUGGING AN OFFICE Checking an office for phone taps and electronic bugging devices takes at least four hours for each 5000 square feet of office space (two hours for a sweep using instruments and two hours for a physical search). *Boardroom Reports*

545. PLANTING CORN You need five pounds of corn seed to plant an acre of corn. *Peter van Berkum, Kittery Point, Maine*

546. WASTING ENERGY Most people waste 30 to 50 percent of the energy they use without ever realizing it. *Fred Langa, senior editor, New Shelter magazine*

547. USING DOGS TO CARRY PACKS A dog can comfortably carry half his weight in a backpack. Working dogs can carry up to twice their body weight for short periods.
Alwyn T. Perrin, Explorers Ltd. Source Book

548. SCUBA DIVING For practical reasons and safety, 100 feet is usually considered to be the maximum depth for sport diving.
Jack T. Marshall, professional diving instructor, Trumansburg, New York

549. PLAYING POOL In a game of eight ball, let your opponent sink half his balls before you sink your first. That way, your balls will interfere with his shooting but his balls won't be there to interfere with your shooting. *John Lilly, mechanical engineer*

550. RUNNING A RACE Five percent of your total training mileage in the last eight weeks before a race equals your personal breaking point in a race.
Jeff Furman, business consultant

551. FLYING IN CROSSWINDS Most light planes are capable of taking off or landing in 90-degree crosswinds that are less than 20 percent of the airplane's power-off stall speed.
Gene Miller, engineer

552. MANAGING AN APIARY One skilled person can manage five hundred bee colonies.
Jeff Furman, business consultant

553. RAISING BEEF One person can take care of up to two hundred cattle.
Pat Woodruff, television repairman

554. RUNNING A DAIRY You need one person for every thirty cows to run a self-sufficient dairy farm.
Chris Dahl, dairy farmer

555. THE BEEF CARCASS RULE OF ONE-QUARTER A properly butchered beef carcass is one-quarter steaks, one-quarter ground beef and stew meat, one-quarter roasts, and one-quarter waste.
Harry Pound, Pound's Meat Cutting

556. PLAYING POKER After the deal, a player who stays in the game and plays out more than one hand in five is overstraining the law of averages and is on his way to the poorhouse.
Dale Armstrong, card player

557. SPOTTING A BAD CHECK There are three signs of a phony check. (1) The printing is shiny when held up to light. (2) None of the edges is perforated. (3) The check number is between 100 and 150 (new bank accounts are responsible for nine out of ten bad checks).
Israeloff, Trattner & Co., CPAs, Valley Stream, New York

558. CASTRATING CALVES Castrate a calf when his testicles are the size of a squirrel's head.
Jim Crissman, veterinary pathologist, Cornell University

559. LOBSTER TAILS A lobster tail should always curl. If this does not happen, the lobster is dead or dying. If the tail does not curl on a boiled lobster, the lobster was dead before it was boiled.
T. M. Prudden, lobster expert

560. BUYING A BICYCLE LOCK The lighter the bicycle, the heavier the lock should be.
Karen Missavage, Birmingham, Michigan

561. LOSING YOUR MONEY You should drop out of a poker game when you have lost more than twenty times the maximum bet allowed in the game.
Edwin Silberstang, games expert

562. DIGGING A WELL BY HAND It is difficult and dangerous to hand-dig a narrow hole with vertical sides. If you are digging a surface well by hand, make the top of your hole three times the width you hope to have at the bottom.
Harlan Cooke, cattle hauler

563. CHOPPING WOOD Most people who try chopping a tree with an axe soon discover that the axe will wedge in the wood if the cut is not made wide enough. In most cases, the width of the chop area should be as wide as the tree is thick.
Peter van Berkum, Kittery Point, Maine

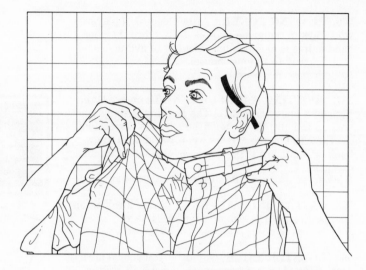

564. BUYING NEW PANTS   You can check the fit of new pants without trying them on. With the top of the pants closed and the button snapped, the waistband should just wrap around your neck.
Harvey Ferdschneider, photographer

565. GRAZING A HORSE   Provide at least one acre of good pasture per horse.
Clarence Morgan, The Morgan Palomino Ranch

566. TRYING A NEW IDEA   It takes three tries to get a new idea right, especially if a physical prototype is involved. The first try reveals any obvious shortcomings, and the second try cleans these up so you can see what you really need to do.
J. Baldwin, designer and writer

567. SUBMITTING A SEALED BID   In a reserve bid auction, the seller reserves the right to place one last bid after the other bids are opened. In other words, the seller has a price below which he or she will not sell. Instead of announcing that price before the auction, it is a common practice for the auctioneer to list the high and low end of the bids he or she expects to get. You can usually assume that the seller's reserve bid is about two thirds of the lower estimate.   *Katherine Havens, antique dealer*

568. MAKING MAPLE SYRUP   It takes about one hundred maple trees to make twenty-five gallons of syrup.   *Stephen Pitkin, maple syrup maker*

569. PLANTING CORN   Plant corn when the oak leaves are the size of squirrel's ears.
Penelope Wickham, marketing director

570. GROWING PLANTS UNDER LIGHTS   You need at least twenty watts of fluorescent light for every square foot of growing area.
Amy Rice, College Park, Maryland

571. BUYING A WORD PROCESSOR   A word processor triples office typing speed. It is time to buy one when your secretarial staff spends more than 20 percent of its time retyping.
Randy J. Goldfield, Gibbs Consulting Group, New York City

572. FOLLOWING THE FOOD CHAIN   Different levels in the food chain are called trophic levels. As organisms eat and get eaten, food energy is passed along the food chain. From one trophic level to the next, there is a 90-percent loss of energy.
M. N., Enterprise, Oregon

573. CHEMICAL REACTIONS   Plan on a 10-percent loss of material for each step in a sequential chemical reaction.
David Finn, printmaker, New York City

574. SILK-SCREEN PRINTING   Some serigraphs or silk-screen prints are smudged or damaged during production. You can plan on losing 10 percent of an edition each time you add a color.
David Finn, printmaker, New York City

575. MAKING CONCRETE   It takes one person the better part of a day to mix and pour 2 cubic yards of concrete.   *Ken Kern, writer and builder*

576. CLIMBING MOUNT EVEREST   The death rate for climbers on Mount Everest is one for every seven to make it to the top. The rate is lower for Sherpas and women, higher for military people.
David A. Lloyd-Jones, Tokyo, Japan

577. LIFTING WEIGHTS FOR EXERCISE Your pulse rate while lifting weights shouldn't exceed the maximum rate you can tolerate while running or doing aerobic exercises. *Health Letter, San Antonio, Texas*

578. CHEMICAL REACTIONS The rate of a chemical reaction doubles for every 10-degree Centigrade rise in temperature. *Ken Partymiller, chemist*

579. BIOCHEMICAL REACTIONS The reaction rate in a biochemical system doubles for every 10-degree Centigrade rise in temperature within the limits of enzyme viability.
Pierre Gremaud, Waitsfield, Vermont

580. TALKING TO REPORTERS Don't tell a reporter anything you don't want printed. Not that they can't be trusted, but what you tell reporters off the record can lead them to another source who may not be so discreet. *Lester R. Bittel, management consultant*

TOM PARKER
BOX 198, RD 1
ALPINE, N.Y.
14805

581. USING A CHAINSAW Plan on spending half an hour of maintenance for each two hours of chainsaw use.
Rob Weinberg, Tassajara Zen Mountain Center, Carmel Valley, California

582. LEARNING TO READ You can teach your children how to find books at their own reading level. Tell your child to open a book near the middle and read from the top of any full page. If there are five words the child doesn't know before getting to the end of the page, the book is too hard.
Eliza Brownrigg Graue, Is Your Child Gifted?

583. MEASURING GOOD WILL If you plan to buy a going retail store, you should compare as many factors as possible. As opposed to variables such as location, size, and accessibility, public good will or reputation is hard to measure. One rule is to consider the store's profits for the last three to five years, minus the owner's salary, to be a measure of the owner's good will.
Bram Cavin, florist, How to Run a Successful Florist and Plant Store

584. NEGOTIATING   If you are negotiating for money, pay careful attention to the increments of change in your opponent's demands. When the increments begin to decrease in size, your opponent is reaching his or her bargaining limit.
Jeff Furman, business consultant

585. CUTTING FIREWOOD   One person, working alone, can cut, haul, and stack about a cord of firewood a day.   *John Fay, apple grower*

586. BOILING MAPLE SAP   It takes a cord of wood to boil down one thousand gallons of maple sap.
Stephen Pitkin, maple syrup maker

587. BOILING MAPLE SAP   It takes about forty gallons of maple sap to make a gallon of maple syrup.
Rick Eckstrom, builder

588. KNITTING   Allow 1 inch of yarn for every stitch you want to cast on your needle.
M. N., Enterprise, Oregon

589. BUYING CAR PARTS   A used car part should cost no more than 60 percent of the new part list price. A used mechanical or electrical part should go for half the rebuilt and one-quarter the new price.
LeRoi Smith, writer and car builder

590. TECHNICAL PROJECTS RULE OF TWO
Complex technical projects always take twice as long to finish as your most thorough and conservative estimate, even when you've used this rule and doubled your first estimate.   *Robert Cumberford, Austin, Texas*

591. LOSING A LOVED ONE   It takes five years to recover from the death of a beloved spouse.
Penny Russell, artist, Sewickley, Pennsylvania

592. GOING INTO DERMATOLOGY   You need one dermatologist for every forty thousand people.
Dr. Robert Horn, dermatologist

DEAR TOM,
HERE'S A RULE OF THUMB THAT DEVELOPED WHEN FALCONERS BEGAN TO USE SCALES IN MANAGING THEIR BIRDS.
    WHEN HANDLING A FRESH PASSAGE FALCON (BIRD OF THE YEAR, TRAPPED IN THE FALL), BRING THE BIRD'S WEIGHT DOWN 10% FROM THE FRESHLY TRAPPED WEIGHT; MANNING (TAMING) AND TRAINING WILL PROCEED MUCH FASTER.
WHEN THE BIRD IS TAME AND STEADY, THE ORIGINAL WEIGHT IS OFTEN A GOOD WEIGHT AT WHICH THE FALCON CAN BE FLOWN.
            BEST REGARDS,
            DOUG PINEO

RULE OF THUMB:
TO FIND OUT HOW MANY LIGHTS YOUR XMAS TREE NEEDS, MULTIPLY TREE HEIGHT TIMES TREE WIDTH TIMES THREE: MERRY, MERRY! MICHAEL SPENCER, LAWYER

NORTHERN CALIFORNIA COAST
Miles of rugged photogenic beauty provides visitors with year around fishing, exploring, beach combing, driftwood collecting, picnic sites and camping.
BI2467

ADDRESS
TOM PARKER
BOX 198 Rd 1
ALPINE
NY 14805

A goat -- any goat -- can be relied upon to do the opposite of what you want it to do.

            Dick Ketchum
            Richard M. Ketchum, editor
            Box 870
            Manchester Center, Vt. 05255

FEB. 20TH '83
TOM:
HAVE ADMIRED YOUR ARTWORK ■ OVER THE YEARS MAY YOU DO SOME TIGHT STUFF! HERE'S A RULE OF THUMB FOR ARTISTS:

"ANYTHING THAT WORKS!"

—R. CRUMB '83

593. BUILDING A STONE WALL   You should plan on ordering (or collecting) 2 cubic yards of stone for every cubic yard of finished wall.
David Finn, printmaker and stonemason, Boston, Massachusetts

594. CARING FOR A CHRISTMAS TREE   A Christmas tree should be taken down on St. Valentine's day or when it is bald, whichever comes first.
Shelley Mosher, Groton, New York

595. MAKING A MOVIE   The smallest letters in a title should be at least one-twenty-fifth the height of the screen.   *Scott Marsh, photographer*

596. FOLLOWING A WARM FRONT   Warm fronts usually move slower than fifteen miles per hour, and about half the speed of cold fronts.
Stephen Friends, meteorologist

597. SQUEEZING THROUGH A HOLE   If a caver can get his head through a tight spot, the rest of his body will go through, too. However, this assumes that the passage is at least a yard wide and is really tight for 8 inches or less.   *David R. McClurg, speleologist*

598. HOLES FOR RATS   A grown rat can pass through a hole the size of a quarter.
Whetstone, Lafayette, Louisiana

599. WEARING CONTACT LENSES   It takes your eyes a number of weeks to adjust to wearing contact lenses. In most cases, it will take about one week for each year you have been wearing glasses.
Irene Fudge, lab technician

600. ACCEPTING AN ENGAGEMENT RING   The cost of an engagement ring was once considered to be an important gauge of a gentleman's character. A smart young lady would look for a suitor who spent one month's wages on a ring. Any young man who spent less than a month's salary on a ring was most likely cheap; one who spent more was a showoff.
Adam Perl, antique dealer

601. TAKING PICTURES INTO THE SUN When you are shooting subjects into the sun, open the aperture an extra one and a half f-stops.
John Reis, photographer

602. CHOOSING AN ARROW To quickly estimate the arrow length best for you, hold the end of a yardstick against your breast bone with your hands together stretched in front of you. Read the arrow length where your fingertips touch the yardstick.
Dana Burdick, electronic technician

603. CHOOSING AN ARROW To quickly estimate the arrow length best for you, take 38 percent of the distance between your fingertips with your arms extended sideways.
Cliff Burns, bow hunter

604. WALKING ON ICE Blue ice is safer than black ice.   *Cally Arthur, Baltimore, Maryland*

605. SERVING WINE There are six glasses of wine in a bottle.   *Tom Werner, Athens, Georgia*

606. RAISING BEEF A properly fed beef cow should gain two or three pounds a day.
Pat Woodruff, television repairman

607. CARRYING THINGS You can lift, for a short time, twice your weight. You can carry and move your own weight. For a long distance you can carry, uncomfortably, half your weight, or comfortably, one-fourth your weight.   *J. Baldwin, designer and writer*

608. RAIN Rain before 7:00, done by 11:00.
Steve Ramsey, antiquarian

609. SHOOTING AT DUCKS It is usually safe to assume that if you are missing shots at crossing birds you are shooting behind them.
Nelson Bryant, The New York Times

610. CONTROLLING A WILDFIRE Assuming you can get to it within ten minutes, a one-acre wild-fire with fuel moisture at 4 percent or less will burn forty acres before it can be controlled.
Gerald Myers, Redway, California

611. SCUBA DIVING Scuba divers use a belt with lead weights to adjust their buoyancy in the water. The average diver will need 10 percent of his or her body weight in extra lead.
Jack T. Marshall, professional diving instructor, Trumansburg, New York

612. SHOPPING AT GARAGE SALES Garage sales are good places to shop. As a rule, half the things for sale are underpriced. However, keep in mind that a quarter of the things for sale are probably overpriced.   *George Perfect, antiques dealer*

613. ARC WELDING The length of your arc determines the quality of your weld. A good arc sounds like frying bacon. An arc that's too long starts to hiss and sound hollow; an arc that's too short stops arcing.
Smokey Olsen, Lawrenceburg, Indiana

614. ARC WELDING Welders often need to quickly estimate the amount of welding rod they need to join two pieces of metal along a seam, or bead, as the finished weld is called. As a rule, the length of the rod equals the length of the bead.
Rick Eckstrom, builder

615. STARTING AN APIARY No sizable apiary should be placed within two miles of another.
Dan Kaiser, Roanoke, Virginia

616. BUYING CLOTHES A garment is probably well made if stripes or plaids are matched at the seams. The more seams that match the better the garment.
Stephanie Judy, writer, British Columbia, Canada

617. FLYING INTO LOW PRESSURE High to low, look out below. If you fly from an area of high barometric pressure to an area of low barometric pressure without adjusting your altimeter, it will read higher than your actual altitude.   *Beverly Dunn, pilot*

618. PLANTING CORN IN INDIANA Getting your corn in late is costly. You lose a bushel an acre a day for every day you wait after May 10.
Steve Bruns, farmer

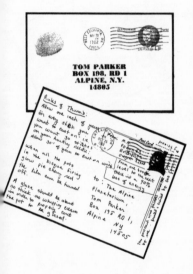

619. WEARING TREAD A pair of shoes is good for 1000 miles. A pair of bicycle tires is good for 4000 miles. *Kevin Kelly, Athens, Georgia*

620. CALLIGRAPHY The most pleasing height for lower-case italic letters is five times the width of the penpoint, or nib. *Ashley Miller, calligrapher*

621. GLAZING POTTERY Dividing a pot in half with a glaze makes it weaker visually.
Corinne Abbott, Manitou Springs, Colorado

622. DESIGNING A ROOF When you are planning a house, make the angle of the roof noticeably more or noticeably less than a right angle; otherwise, the appearance is depressing.
Susan Pitkin, librarian

623. GROWING CHRISTMAS TREES You can plan on eventually harvesting four to five hundred Christmas trees for every one thousand seedlings you plant. *Jay Waring, tree grower and plant specialist*

624. SETTING YOUR RATES Free-lance artists and graphic designers should determine their hourly rate by dividing their annual income requirements by one thousand. *Mike Rider, art director*

625. RUNNING A DAIRY The average dairy farmer spends half his time milking or doing chores related to milking. *William Stillman, dairy farmer*

626. BUYING HARDWARE Ordinary hardware, like tools, bikes, lawnmowers, and cars, costs about $3.50 to $4.00 per pound in 1982 dollars. This figure represents the approximate cost of manufacture and marketing. Hardware that costs more is either high precision or overpriced.
J. Baldwin, designer and writer

627. INSPECTING A DEAD DEER Check the bone marrow of a deer's thighbone. If it resembles red or yellow jelly, the deer starved to death. If the marrow is solid fat, flecked with a little red, or even red but still solid, the deer was well fed.
Paul Kelsey, biologist

628. THINGS THAT BITE   As a matter of biology rather than sexism, if something bites you, it is probably female.
Scott M. Kruse, Yosemite National Park, California

629. CLEANING A PARK   The number of people and the amount of litter decrease with the cube of the vertical distance and the square of the horizontal distance to the trailhead.
Scott M. Kruse, Yosemite National Park, California

630. ESTIMATING YOUR ADULT HEIGHT   Your adult height will be twice your height at the age of twenty-two months.
Steve Parker, aerospace engineer, Princeton, New Jersey

631. ESTIMATING YOUR ADULT HEIGHT   Your adult height will be twice your height at the age of three.
Douglas Kellog, Washington, D.C.

632. MEASURING CHILDREN   The height of a child on its second birthday will be about half its adult height, though girls will be a little shorter when grown.
J. Eichelberger, Alameda, California

633. FINDING DIRECTIONS   Swallows build their nests under the eaves on the south side of buildings. Sometimes they will use the east side, but they never use the north.
Alwyn T. Perrin, editor, Explorers Ltd. Source Book

634. TELLING SHEEP FROM GOATS   Some breeds of sheep look like goats and some breeds of goats look like sheep. In general, sheep's tails hang down and goats' tails stand up.
Mary Ellen Parker, teacher, Cincinnati, Ohio

635. CHECKING HENS   You can tell whether a hen is laying eggs or not by sizing her cloaca with your fingers. If one finger fits in her cloaca, she's not laying; if two fingers fit, she might be; if three fingers fit, she's laying for sure.
Peter van Berkum, Kittery Point, Maine

636. HITCHING YOUR DOG TO A SLED   One
medium-sized dog in good condition, but a bit out of
shape (like most pets), can easily pull a fair-sized child
on a sled; two dogs can pull a child and an adult.
Alwyn T. Perrin, Explorers Ltd. Source Book

637. BUILDING A POND FOR LIVESTOCK   A
pond supplied entirely by surface water should be
built to hold at least six times the amount of water
you need for your livestock.
Carl S. Winkelblech, New York State extension agent

638. DITCHING AN AIRPLANE OVER WATER
If you are making an emergency landing on water in a land plane, study the pattern of waves and swells on the surface. At all costs, avoid landing into the face of a swell. If you have to land perpendicular to a swell, touch down on the top or back side.

J. T. Schaefer, pilot

639. STOPPING A CAR   If you can't see the rear tires of the car in front of you at a stoplight, you're too close.   *Anonymous British driving student*

640. STOPPING A CAR   If you can't see the license plate of the car in front of you at a stoplight, you're too close.   *James Vincent, driver education instructor*

641. STOPPING A CAR   If you can't read the odometer of the car in front of you at a stoplight, you're too far back.
Henning Pape, taxi driver, West Berlin, Germany

642. CHOOSING PAPER FOR BROCHURES
Men respond best to smooth, coated paper; women respond best to textured, uncoated paper.
Anne Trovinger, graphic designer

643. PLANNING A POND   The value of a finished pond is roughly three times the cost of constructing it.   *Tim Matson, writer and pond maker*

644. FOLLOWING AIR MASSES   Air masses travel about 750 miles per day (slower in summer, faster in winter).   *Eric Sloane, artist and writer*

645. RUNNING A FACTORY   A normal parts or machinery factory will produce $115,000 per employee per year. A well-run plant will produce $250,000 per employee. There are many exceptions to this, though. The "value added" to the finished product, exclusive of the cost of materials, supplies, packaging, and overhead, should be $70,000 per person, or you don't have a business.   *David A. Lloyd-Jones, Tokyo, Japan*

646. PLANTING SEEDS   Most seeds should be set as deep as they are wide.
Peter van Berkum, Kittery Point, Maine

647. PLANTING SEEDS Never plant a seed deeper than twice its width.
Jim Allen, Creekside Nursery, Santa Rosa, California

648. SELLING INVENTIONS Less than one patented invention in a hundred makes any money for the inventor.
Scott Parker, Beaumont, Texas

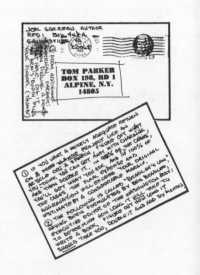

649. THE GRADE SCHOOL RULE OF FIVE Subtract five from the age of a child to determine his or her grade in school. Conversely, add five to the grade of a child to determine his or her age. A fourth-grader, for instance, is usually nine years old.
Pat Howard, teacher

650. LOOKING AT THINGS UNDER WATER Because of refraction, underwater objects viewed through a flat face mask or camera port appear about 25 percent larger and closer.
Jack T. Marshall, professional diving instructor, Trumansburg, New York

651. USING A PAINT ROLLER The average paint roller will apply 2 to 3 square feet of paint per dip.
Rick Eckstrom, builder

652. CAPTURING SOMETHING ON FILM If you want to capture something on film but you can't take several exposures, overexpose the metered value by one-half to one f-stop. The information has a better chance of being recorded.
Carl Ebeling, engineer, Pittsburgh, Pennsylvania

653. HERDING SHEEP Indian shepherds plan on using three and a half acres of desert land for each sheep they graze.
Roger Peterson, Phoenix, Arizona

654. MAKING COFFEE FOR LARGE GROUPS A one-pound can of regular grind, tossed into a commercial urn, will brew fifty cups of decent coffee or sixty cups of weak coffee. A pound and a half of regular grind will make ninety cups of decent coffee.
John Brink, building superintendent, Masonic Temple

655. BUYING ARTICHOKES Fresh artichokes squeak when rubbed together.
Sunny Lenz, New Canton, Virginia

656. DRIVING ON ICE AND SNOW Second gear is the best one for driving on ice and snow.
Leslie Warren, music teacher, Kittery Point, Maine

657. EXERCISING Never exercise so hard that you are gasping for breath. In fact, never do anything so hard that you are gasping for breath.
Byron Roth, biochemist

658. SHOPPING FOR THINGS It will take twenty to thirty minutes to shop for one item if you know exactly what you want and where to go. Thus, if you go out at lunch to buy three different things, plan on being gone for one to one and a half hours.
Jim Kauffold, Belmont, California

659. SADDLING A HORSE Check your stirrup length from a mounted, standing position. Stirrups are properly adjusted if you can just fit the palm of your hand between your crotch and the saddle.
Stacey DiGiovani, equestrian

660. STARTING A BUSINESS VENTURE The idea for a new venture is likely to be strategically unsound if it can't be put into one coherent sentence.
Kenichi Ohmae, The Mind of the Strategist

661. THE MARKETING RULE OF THREE Any new product should have at least three easily recognizable advantages over its competition.
Lloyd Barringer, sales representative

662. DOING THINGS Find two good reasons to do something; you can always find one good reason to do anything.
Michael Mangan, stained-glass designer

663. COURT TRIALS Anytime a district attorney brings a defendant to trial, he or she is convinced that the defendant is guilty even though proving it may be impossible. *Anonymous lawyer, Chicago, Illinois*

664. SETTING UP A LOBSTER TANK Provide at least two gallons of refrigerated water per pound of lobster.
T. M. Prudden, lobster expert

665. FEEDING PIGS Never feed pigs viney plants — it gives them the itch.
Clayton Mitstifer, machinist, Cayutaville, New York

666. FEEDING CATS Feed your cat as much as it will eat in thirty minutes, two times a day.
Ronald Newberry, gardener

667. FEEDING A PARKING METER Always feed a parking meter with the smallest denomination coins you have. You will almost always get more time for your money if you use pennies instead of dimes. And, if the meter jams, you win big.
Gerald Gutlipp, mathematician

668. HANGING UP A TELEPHONE Telephone salespeople should always let the customer hang up first. Jumping the gun can cut off a last minute add-on order.
Januz Direct Marketing Letter, Lake Forest, Illinois

669. REPEATING AN EXPERIMENT If you can't repeat your own experiment, you are probably not doing science. If no one else can repeat your experiment, you are probably lying.
Gary Marlow, scientist, Ithaca, New York

670. SMOKING LEATHER Leather that has been exposed to smoke won't stiffen after getting wet. The longer the leather is smoked, the darker it becomes — a light buckskin brown indicates that the skin is smoked just the right amount.
Larry Dean Olsen, survival instructor, <u>Outdoor Survival Skills</u>

671. CLIMBING WITHOUT SUPPLEMENTARY OXYGEN I need one week to acclimate my body for climbing a 5000-meter mountain without oxygen, two weeks for a 6000-meter mountain, three for 7000 meters, and at least four weeks for an 8000-meter mountain.
Reinhold Messner, mountaineer, via Henning Pape, West Berlin, Germany

672. FINANCING A MAGAZINE The price of ads in a commercial magazine should be twelve times the printing costs per unit area, including film, separation, and production charges.
David A. Lloyd-Jones, Tokyo, Japan

673. DRYING HERBS It takes about four pounds of fresh herbs to make one pound of dry herbs.
Amy Rice, College Park, Maryland

674. MANAGING THINGS No manager or supervisor should have responsibility for more than six separate activities.   *Lester R. Bittel, management consultant*

675. PANNING A SCENE You should scan, or "pan," a scene with a moving camera no faster than one frame-width per five seconds. In other words, you need to allow at least five seconds for an object entering one side of the screen to pass out the other side.
Christopher Wordsworth, film maker

676. FREEZING FISH You should keep fatty fish frozen for a maximum of three months and lean fish for a maximum of six months. Shellfish should be frozen for no more than one to three months, depending on the type.   *Kenn and Pat Oberrecht, commercial fishers*

677. FENCING LIVESTOCK An electric fence should be three quarters of the shoulder height of the animals it is to enclose.
Carla Corin, biologist, Eagle River, Alaska

678. FILMING A SCENE Purely as a guide, ten seconds is quite a long shot and three seconds is quite a short one. *Christopher Wordsworth, film maker*

679. RUNNING A LAUNDRY IN JAPAN Coin laundry machines must run nine times a day to be profitable in Tokyo. In rural Japan, five or six times a day will do. *David A. Lloyd-Jones, Tokyo, Japan*

680. SEEING IN THE DARK It takes fifteen minutes for the human iris to open to its widest extent and another half-hour to forty-five minutes for the retina behind the iris to become adjusted for good night vision. *Vinson Brown, vision expert*

681. CHOOSING A CANOE PADDLE To check a canoe paddle for size, stand it on the ground in front of you. The handle should come to the height of your chin if you plan to paddle from the bow of the canoe; it should come to the height of your eye if you plan to paddle from the stern.
Peter van Berkum, Kittery Point, Maine

682. SHOPLIFTING You can figure that one out of every forty to sixty people in a store is a shoplifter. Only one in every two hundred shoplifters gets caught.
Eugene A. Sloane, security expert

683. A MOUSE IN YOUR HOUSE If you see one mouse in your house, you probably have a dozen.
C. A. Lacey, town historian, Richford, New York

684. CALORIES AND JOGGING Jogging burns about 100 calories per mile.
J. Benze, plumber's apprentice

685. SWARMING BEES Honeybees will start to congregate in a horseshoe-shaped pattern on the front of the hive three days before they start to swarm.
Anthony Sykes, orchard worker

686. WRITING A BOOK To determine how long it will take to write a book, figure out how long it should take, double it and add six months.
Ben Bradlee, executive editor, The Washington Post, via Joel Garreau

687. HITCHHIKING IN AFRICA Allow one week to hitchhike a thousand kilometers in Africa.
Henning Pape, traveler, West Germany

688. MEASURING MICE There are approximately 250 mice to the gallon.
Lecki Ord, Melbourne, Australia

689. SCHEDULING WORK According to F. P. Brooks, author of *The Mythical Man-Month*, anyone developing a new computer system should allow one third of the time for design and planning, one sixth for programming, one fourth for testing components, and one fourth for testing the system as a whole.
Clifton Royston, programmer/analyst, Nukualofa, Tonga

690. BUYING STOCK Don't maintain an undiversified portfolio, one with fewer than seven stocks in it. You're better off with ten go-go stocks than with one blue chip, as people who bought General Public Utilities found out when the Three Mile Island accident happened. If you have less than $15,000, diversify through mutual funds.
The American Association of Individual Investors

691. BUYING STOCK Don't buy preferred stocks, other than convertibles. They're good buys for corporations because of the dividend exclusion, but individuals get better yields from bonds.
The American Association of Individual Investors

692. BUYING STOCK Don't move a substantial portion of your wealth into or out of the market at one time. Ease in, ease out.
The American Association of Individual Investors

693. BUYING STOCK Don't buy common stock with money you feel that you will need in less than four years.
The American Association of Individual Investors

694. BUYING STOCK Don't buy stock that is included in the Fortune 500 or Standard & Poor's 500. The chances of such stocks being undervalued are virtually nil.
The American Association of Individual Investors

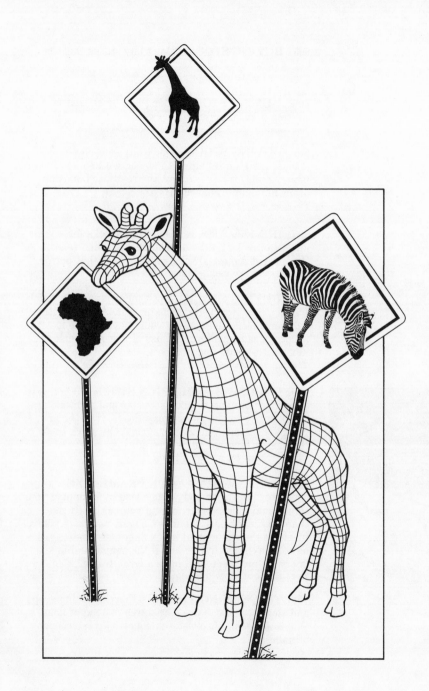

695. BUYING STOCK Don't buy stocks that are being pushed by a broker.
The American Association of Individual Investors

696. BUYING STOCK Don't buy stock that is getting a lot of play in the press.
The American Association of Individual Investors

697. BUYING STOCK Don't buy safe, low-risk stocks. Instead, buy growth stocks with some of your money and, for balance, put the rest into bonds or other minimum-risk securities.
The American Association of Individual Investors

698. BUYING STOCK Don't buy stocks for a year after a presidential inauguration. For some reason, the market almost always goes down in that period.
The American Association of Individual Investors

699. BUYING STOCK Don't follow anyone's "infallible system" for beating the market. Anyone with a system that really worked would never share it with others because widespread use of it would cause the market to adjust and nullify it.
The American Association of Individual Investors

700. CHOOSING A SHOTGUN STOCK When you snap your shotgun to your shoulder and sight along the barrel, you should see only the bead at the end. If you have to jam your cheek against the stock to do this, something has to be altered.
Nelson Bryant, The New York Times

701. DETERMINING YOUR FRAME SIZE You can determine your body frame size by wrapping your thumb and index finger around your wrist. If the thumb extends past the index finger, you have a small frame; if the thumb and index finger just meet, you have an average frame; and if the thumb and index finger do not meet, you have a large frame.
Terry Hayward, medical technician

702. THICKENING THINGS For thickening soups and sauces, you can use cornstarch instead of flour. One tablespoon of cornstarch equals two tablespoons of flour.
Kay Parker, quilt designer

703. SLEEPING WITH A BABY Most babies will sleep through the night after reaching a weight of eleven pounds or an age of six weeks, whichever comes first.
Linda McCandless, shepherd

704. SLEEPING WITH A BABY Most babies will sleep through the night at eight weeks of age, or three months of age, one or the other.
Louise Mudrak, ecologist

705. TRAVELING ON FOOT There is a simple test for checking your pace: If you can't keep it up, hour after hour, it is too fast.
Peggy Kerber, editor, Mountaineering

706. BUYING SKI BOOTS Properly fitting cross-country ski boots should feel like bedroom slippers.
Gordon Burt, ski instructor

707. ASSURING SUCCESS To succeed against all possible odds, count on at least one in four things going wrong. In other words, you need a 33-percent margin of safety. If you have to have thirty of something, plan to make forty.
Stanley J. Goodman, How to Manage a Turnaround

708. BETTING ON A HORSE If you don't have much information before a race, bet on a horse that is swishing his tail straight up and down.
Donald Mycrantz, Tulsa, Oklahoma

709. PARTICIPATING IN A TRADE SHOW A trade show visitor will stop at about twenty booths per trade show. The average stop lasts about fifteen minutes, so keep your demonstrations to less than ten minutes to allow time for conversation.
Exhibits Surveys, Inc., Middletown, New Jersey

710. WORKING OVERTIME After working eight hours per day or forty-eight hours per week, it takes about three overtime hours to produce two standard hours' worth of results. For heavy work, count on two hours' time for each hours' worth of output.
Illinois Institute of Technology

711. PLANNING A NEWS BROADCAST A half-hour network news broadcast reduced to type will fill about half the front page of a newspaper.
Roger Carpenter, news buff

712. SCULPTING WITH PAPER You can sculpt a full-size likeness of two five-year-old kids from one copy of the Sunday *New York Times*, if you save the *Book Review* for yourself.
David Finn, printmaker, New York City

713. DEFENDING YOURSELF   If you are attacked by several people at once, go for the largest and put one or both of his or her eyes out. This will produce sufficient consternation in the others to give you time to flee.   *Peter Garrison, writer and pilot*

714. CHECKING YOUR PULSE   The normal resting pulse rate for humans is about equal to the external temperatures they find most comfortable measured in degrees Fahrenheit — 68 to 72.
J. Eichelberger, Alameda, California

715. HEAVY TRAFFIC   Unless someone screws up, heavy traffic tends to keep itself at a speed of about twenty-two miles per hour, the speed that allows the most cars to use a road at once.
John Schubert, senior editor, Bicycling magazine

716. THE RULE OF 80-20   According to Alan Lakein, author of *How to Get Control of Your Time and Your Life,* 80 percent of the benefit comes from 20 percent of the effort. So, by choosing carefully, you can do 20 percent of the jobs in front of you and reap 80 percent of the benefit of doing them all. Similarly, 80 percent of your phone calls go to 20 percent of the numbers you use; 80 percent of your meals use 20 percent of your recipes.
Ray Bruman, Berkeley, California

717. THE CONTRIBUTION RULE OF 80-20   Generally, 20 percent of the contributors account for 80 percent of the funds.
Edwin Ted Kaehler, Mountain View, California

718. THE MANUFACTURING RULE OF 80-20   As a rule, 20 percent of a product line produces 80 percent of the profit.
Cynthia Orr, consulting geophysicist, El Paso, Texas

719. PARKING CARS   One acre will park a hundred cars.   *E. Mankin, journalist, Venice, California*

720. MAKING MAPLE SYRUP   Obviously, the amount of syrup you get depends on the number of taps you put into trees. You can plan on one quart of finished syrup per tap per season.
Caroline Eckstrom, managing editor

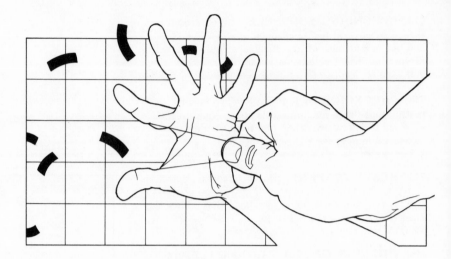

721. CHOOSING A BOW A beginning archer should be able to hold a bow fully drawn for ten seconds without his or her arm shaking. An experienced archer should be able to hold a bow at full draw for fifteen or twenty seconds before starting to shake.
Cliff Burns, bow hunter

722. RIDING A BICYCLE LONG DISTANCE To avoid burning out when riding for distances of fifty miles or more, climb steep hills in lower gears. It is a good practice to estimate the highest possible gear you could use and divide it by two.
David L. Smith, M.D., Middlesboro, Kentucky

723. STARTING A FOOD CO-OP Except in remote rural areas, fifteen to twenty-five households should form enough of a buying pool to begin collectively ordering some produce, grain, and cheese.
The Co-op Handbook Collective, The Food Co-op Handbook

724. CHECKING THE ICE FOR SKATING One inch, keep away; two inches, one may; three inches, small groups; four inches, O.K.   *Holley Bailey, editor*

725. KEEPING A HORSE If you can't afford better fencing than barbed wire, you can't afford a horse.
Clarence Morgan, Morgan Palomino Ranch

726. KEEPING LOBSTERS HEALTHY Lobsters are very susceptible to chemicals and aerosol sprays used in the vicinity of tanks. As a rule, anything that will kill a fly will kill a lobster more quickly.
T. M. Prudden, lobster expert

727. USING YOUR BRAINS In a pinch, you can tan a skin with the brain of the animal that provides the skin. The brains are mashed and rubbed into the hide with a smooth rock. Conveniently, one deer brain is enough to tan one deer skin and one mouse brain is enough to tan one mouse skin.
Larry Dean Olsen, survival instructor, Outdoor Survival Skills

728. HEATING WITH PEOPLE Ten people will raise the temperature of a medium-size room 1 degree per hour.
John Brink, building superintendent, Masonic Temple

729. HEATING WITH PEOPLE According to my roommate in a Swiss boarding school, architects and engineers figure that, as far as heat is concerned, three people equal one radiator.
Helen D. Haller, Ithaca, New York

730. GIVING OFF HEAT People normally produce about 500 BTUs per hour. People who are exercising produce three or four times that much heat.
Brenda Poole, biologist

731. BODY HEAT A resting human gives off as much heat as a 150-watt light bulb. You can use this fact to keep the temperature in a greenhouse constant, even as you come and go. Just turn the light out whenever you go in.
John Schubert, editor, Bicycling magazine

732. TURNING OFF YOUR ENGINE It pays to turn off your engine if it will be idling for more than one minute.
Owen Chambers, petroleum distributor

733. FOOD PRICES A 1-percent shortage of a particular food will cause a 4-percent increase in price.
Richard Elliot, Warwick, Rhode Island

734. MAILING A LETTER   The cost of writing, typing, filing, and mailing a single business letter is close to $4.50. If you can make your point quickly, a long-distance telephone call is usually cheaper than the mail.   *Paul Fargis, independent book producer*

735. PLANNING AN INDEX   Allowing space for an index in a book is no problem once the type has been set and the indexing has been done. But with a new manuscript, you can only guess. As a rule of thumb, allow one page of index to every forty pages of manuscript with average copy, one to thirty for a manuscript with a lot of names or technical terms, one to fifty for one with comparatively few. Check your guess with the editor and use his figure if it differs from yours.   *Marshall Lee, bookmaker*

736. COOKING RICE   To cook rice, rest the tip of your index finger on top of the rice and add enough water to reach the first joint. This works for any size pot.   *E. Mankin, journalist, Venice, California*

737. COOKING RICE   Old Japanese/Hawaiian rule: one knuckle rice, two knuckles water.
Nani Paape, textile designer, Seattle, Washington

738. FILING THINGS   If your office is typical, three quarters of the things in your files should have been placed in your wastebasket.
Edwin C. Bliss, time management expert

739. THE SURVIVAL RULE OF FIFTY   You have a 50 percent chance of surviving for 50 minutes in 50 degree water.   *Rick Eckstrom, builder*

740. INCREASING FARES   The New York Metropolitan Transit Authority needs to raise its fares five cents for every $50 million they go in the hole.
Henning Pape, traveler, West Berlin, Germany

741. FERTILIZING TOMATOES   Fertilize tomatoes for the second time when the first cluster of fruit starts to ripen.   *Peter van Berkum, Kittery Point, Maine*

742. EATING A CANTALOUPE   A cantaloupe is ripe when it has a musky smell at the end opposite the stem.   *Brad Edmondson, editor*

743. ANTIQUE RULE OF THREE   Don't buy a piece of antique furniture if you can find three things wrong with it.   *Adam Perl, antique dealer*

744. ANTIQUE CLOTHING   To minimize damage from handling, acidity, pollution, and light, antique clothing should be hung on display for no more than six weeks.   *Ann Farnham, museum curator*

745. CLIMBING MOUNTAINS   According to the 1952 Everest Expedition, 1 pound added to your boots equals 5 pounds added to your back. Buy the lightest boots that are safe.
David A. Lloyd-Jones, Tokyo, Japan

746. LEADING A SEMINAR   If you are leading a seminar, allow six seconds for a response to your questions. If someone is going to respond they'll do it within six seconds.
Tom Werner, management consultant, Athens, Georgia

747. TYING SHOELACES If one shoelace is loose, you need to retie both.
James McConkey, writer, Trumansburg, New York

748. POLITICAL CAMPAIGNS About 5 to 15 percent of the voters in a local race will cast a vote with no information at all (more if they are nearing the end of a long ballot). You can plan on getting a random half of these votes.
Tom Wilbur, county commissioner, East Lansing, Michigan

749. POLITICAL CAMPAIGNS Tall candidates with short names get elected twice as often as short candidates with long names.
Tom Wilbur, county commissioner, East Lansing, Michigan

750. POLITICAL CAMPAIGNS No political rule of thumb applies to lucky (or unlucky) individuals.
Tom Wilbur, county commissioner, East Lansing, Michigan

751. VOLUNTEER RULE OF 90-20 Twenty percent of the people in volunteer groups do ninety percent of the work.
The Diamond of Psi Upsilon

752. FOLLOWING A RIVER Under normal conditions, the distance that a river will run straight is never greater than ten times its width.
Doug Knowles, guitar maker

753. FLYING A KITE A kite automatically assumes its own zenith. It is difficult, if not impossible, to alter this position. Should you continue to let out string the kite will move longitudinally away from you. In this case, due to the added weight of the string, the kite will be pulled slightly lower.
Tal Streeter, kite builder

754. SQUEEZING AN ORANGE One orange will make half a cup of juice.
The Lansing Methodist Church Women's Society

755. SQUEEZING LIMES An average lime contains about three tablespoons of lime juice (and no lemon juice).
Dave and Moddi McKeown, Pittsburgh, Pennsylvania

756. FIGHTING A FOREST FIRE One trained firefighter with a sharp tool can dig six chains (about 400 feet) of finished fireline, 2 feet wide and down to mineral soil, every day for two weeks.
Ned Bounds, sawyer, Salmon, Idaho

757. RUNNING A MARATHON You should be able to run fifty miles per week on a regular basis before you try running a marathon.
Jeff Furman, business consultant

758. DESIGNING A RACE CAR Race car builders substitute light-weight aluminum for steel whenever possible. When working with aluminum, figure one-third the weight and three times the cost of steel.
Joe Ottati, car builder

759. MAKING COTTAGE CHEESE A gallon of milk will make about a pound of cottage cheese.
Mary Ellen Parker, teacher, Cincinnati, Ohio

760. PACK HORSES Plan on using one pack horse for every 150 pounds of supplies you need to carry.
Jim Stevens, outfitter

761. FEEDING HORSES Grass alone won't feed a hard-working horse. As a rule, a horse needs at least five pounds of grain for every half-day of work.
Kevin Reede, Burlington, Vermont

762. SETTING UP A CHICKEN COOP Provide at least three square feet of floor space for each chicken.
Terry Hayward, medical technician

763. SETTING UP AN OFFICE Provide 250 square feet of floor space for each vice president (200 for middle managers, 175 for clerks).
T. U. Powell, architect

764. BUILDING A LOG CABIN FROM A KIT To estimate the cost of a finished log cabin built from a kit, double the cost of the kit and then add some. By the time you are done, it will cost $30,000 to $35,000 to build a log cabin from a $15,000 kit — and that's if you do the work yourself.
M. Trepkus, builder

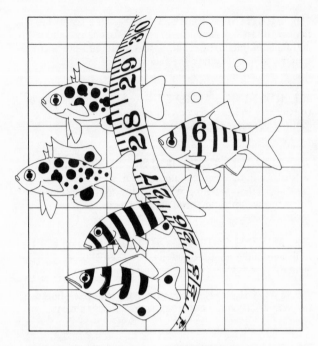

765. SETTING UP AN AQUARIUM Provide at least one gallon of water for each inch of fish.
Jeff Furman, business consultant

766. DRINKING WATER A person should drink at least two quarts of water per day. *Alan Hayes, mover*

767. CHOOSING A RESTAURANT There is one almost infallible way to find honest food at just prices: count the wall calendars in a cafe. No calendar: same as an interstate pit stop. One calendar: preprocessed food assembled in New Jersey. Two calendars: only if fish trophies present. Three calendars: can't miss on the farm-boy breakfasts. Four calendars: try the home-made pie, too. Five calendars: keep it under your hat, or they'll franchise.
William Least Heat Moon, author of Blue Highways

768. RAISING PORK A hog, dressed and hung in the meat locker, will weigh one third of its live weight. *Harry Pound, butcher*

769. MAKING CONTACT PRINTS You should expose your contact prints just long enough to get a solid black print through the clear edge of the film. This will make your good negatives look good and your bad negatives look bad, which saves time later when you are searching for a photo to print.
Mike Rambo, photographer

770. DESIGNING SIGNS AND BILLBOARDS
The letters on a sign or billboard are designed to be readable at a certain distance. Take half the letter height in inches and multiply by 100 to find the readable distance in feet.
Thos. Hodgson, Hodgson Signs, Martha's Vineyard, Massachusetts

771. BATHTUB TOYS Bathtub toys from Singapore generally last longer than those from Taiwan.
Norman Bloom, Calois, Vermont

772. WATCHING WAVES Every seventh wave is a big one.
Annette Arthur, wave watcher

773. KEEPING A FAMILY COW The average family cow needs two acres of good pasture.
Phyllis Wood, press operator, Meriden, Connecticut

774. KEEPING A GUERNSEY COW A good Guernsey cow will produce more than one thousand gallons of whole milk and cream a year. This is enough to feed a family of two adults and three children, with ample skimmed milk left over to feed a veal calf, a pig, and a flock of chickens. An additional bonus is more than fourteen tons of manure for the spreading.
Richard Bacon, writer and historian

775. KEEPING A FAMILY COW A family cow won't pay its keep unless your family needs well over a dollar's worth of butter and milk per day.
Phyllis Wood, press operator, Meriden Connecticut

776. DESIGNING AN AIRPORT A rule of thumb in airport design is to keep walking distances shorter than 2000 feet from gates to baggage.
L. K. Bolef, St. Louis, Missouri

777. LANDSCAPING If you need a four-wheel drive vehicle to get to and maneuver about a worksite, it is probably too wet to work anyway.
Fairleigh Brooks, landscaper, Louisville, Kentucky

778. MAINTAINING YOUR TIRE PRESSURE For every 10-degree drop in temperature, tire pressure goes down one pound.
Peter van Berkum, Kittery Point, Maine

779. GENERATING STEAM Managing flue gases is an important part of generating steam on a large scale. You should plan on one pound of flue gas for every three pounds of steam you generate.
John H. Parker, mechanical engineer

780. SMOKING MARIJUANA Take a hundred milligrams of vitamin C for every bowl of pot you smoke.
Bob Horton, statistics consultant, West Lafayette, Indiana

781. ANALYZING YOUR DIET If your turds float, there's too much fat in your diet.
Michael Rider, art director

782. CONSULTING A consultant should charge at least three times the rate he or she would expect to receive for comparable full-time work with fringe benefits. *John Schubert, senior editor, Bicycling magazine*

783. PLAYING POKER An old rule of thumb says that when your turn comes to call, don't do it — raise or fold. Not always, of course, but amateurs will call a lot more often than professionals.
Dale Armstrong, card player

784. MAKING A PATH If, when removing dirt to make a path of stepping stones, you are vexed by buried rocks, move your path a few feet; somebody else had the same idea fifty or a hundred years before you. *James McConkey, writer, Trumansburg, New York*

785. CHECKING YOUR TIRES Your tire tread should come to the top of Lincoln's head on a penny held on edge upside down. *Barbara Gilbert, bank teller*

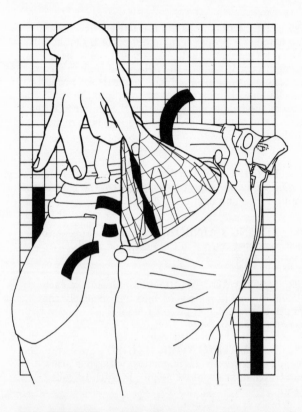

786. FINDING A JOB   Plan on spending one week job hunting for every $2000 in salary and benefits you received in your last job. If your qualifications are particularly high, deduct 20 percent from your search time; if they are low, add 50 percent. If you want to keep your job hunt a secret, multiply your final time by two.   *Robert Half, career consultant and author*

787. FLYING A KITE   Generally, a kite that does not fly straight, does not fly up.
Tal Streeter, kite builder

788. MIXING CONCRETE   The largest stones in a batch of concrete should be one-fourth the thickness of the slab you are going to pour. A driveway 6 inches thick should have stones no larger than one and a half inches in diameter.   *A. D. Elliot, Muncie, Indiana*

789. CHECKING A FIRE LADDER To check a fire ladder for proper lean, stand perfectly erect with the toes against the ladder beam and the arms straight out. If your hands fall on the rung in a comfortable grasping position, the ladder is set properly for climbing. If only the fingertips touch the rung, the base of the ladder is too far from the building. If the heel of the hand touches the rung, the base of the ladder is too close to the building.
The National Fire Protection Association

790. RAISING A LADDER The base of a ladder should be 30 percent of its height from the base of the wall it is leaning against. *Rick Eckstrom, builder*

791. SEEING RAINBOWS Rainbows appear to be east and west, never to the north and south.
Rhiannon, Berkeley, California

792. MACRAMÉ To estimate the length of each strand of cord in a piece of macramé, multiply the length of the finished piece by eight.
Ned Bounds, sawyer, Salmon, Idaho

793. ESTIMATING YOUR HEIGHT As a rule, the distance between your fingertips, with your arms outstretched at shoulder height, is equal to your height.
C. Dees, Stockton, California

794. ADJUSTING THE POINTS ON YOUR CAR In an emergency, you can set the gap on your ignition points by using an ordinary paper match as a feeler gauge. Most matches are about .015 of an inch thick.
Dave Sellers, engineer

795. THINNING TREES FOR LUMBER A trained thinner will use about three quarters of a gallon of fuel and one third of a gallon of bar oil per day, regardless of the number of acres covered.
Ned Bounds, sawyer, Salmon, Idaho

796. BUYING EGGS If the difference in price between medium and large eggs is less than eight cents per dozen, the large eggs are a better deal.
Janet Salmons, home economist

797. EATING EGGS Seven quail eggs equal one chicken egg. *Terry Hayward, medical technician*

798. OSTRICH EGGS One ostrich egg will serve twenty-four people for brunch.
The Joy of Cooking

799. SELLING STOLEN PAINTINGS A stolen painting will sell for one tenth of what it would sell for on the open market.
Kat Dalton, artist, Ithaca, New York

800. BUYING RUNNING SHOES To decide how many dollars you should spend on a pair of running shoes, take the number of miles you run each week and multiply it by two. *Diane Gerhart, accountant*

801. TAKING A SHOWER A five-minute shower uses fifteen to twenty gallons of water.
Scott Parker, Beaumont, Texas

802. DRYING FRUIT Only high-quality fruit should be dried. If it is not good enough to eat fresh, it is not good enough to dry.
D. Antoni, Scottsdale, Arizona

803. AVOIDING HIGH VOLTAGES When you are working in the vicinity of high voltage keep 1 foot of distance between you and the power source for each 1000 volts. For instance, stay 13 feet away from a 13,000 volt power source.
Bob Crews, design scientist, Chicago, Illinois

804. STOPPING AN AIRPLANE To determine the speed at which an aircraft begins to hydroplane, multiply the square root of the tire pressure by nine. A light twin-engine plane with a tire pressure of thirty-six pounds will begin hydroplaning about fifty-four knots, which means that aerodynamic braking will be the major source of stopping power above that speed when there is standing water on the runway.
Bruce Landsberg, pilot and writer

805. THE COLD RULE OF THREE It takes three days to get a cold, three days to have a cold, and three days to get over a cold.
Veronica Cunningham, chemist, Plattsburg, New York

806. THE COLD RULE OF TWO If your doctor treats your cold, it will go away in two weeks. If you leave it alone, it will go away in fourteen days.
Gloria Silverstein, trivia maven, Ithaca, New York

807. GETTING A CONSULTING JOB Personal contacts are best for getting consulting jobs. Twenty leads should produce one assignment.
Dr. Jeffrey L. Lant, Jeffrey Lant Associates, Inc., Cambridge, Massachusetts

808. SMOKING HASHISH Good hashish should make you cough on the first hit.
Anonymous hashish smoker, Poplar Ridge, New York

809. PROOFREADING STATISTICS Always expect to find at least one error when you proofread your own statistics. If you don't, you are probably making the same mistake twice.
Cheryl Russell, demographer

810. BUYING A HOUSE Don't pay more than twice your average annual income for a house.
Scott Parker, Beaumont, Texas

811. IDENTIFYING A SEDGE Sedges have edges (round rushes have none).
Scott M. Kruse, Yosemite National Park, California

812. ESTIMATING TIME (PROJECTS) To bring a project in on time, take a well-researched guess at how long it will take and add time for gremlins and hidden variables. Then double your guess and move to the next unit of time. A job that should take an hour will take about two days. A three-day task will take about six weeks. A two-week task takes about four months, and a job that should take two quarters will take about four years.
Mike Burstein, Mill Valley, and Ray Bruman, Berkeley, California

813. CHOOSING A NEIGHBORHOOD You will usually find the more affluent, attractive neighborhoods on the north and west sides of a city; the poorer and more crime-prone neighborhoods will be on the south and east.
David Chapple, electrical contractor, Palo Alto, California

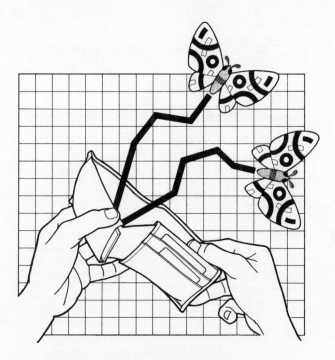

814. PAYING FOR GROCERIES   Figure one
dollar per item to estimate the cost of your groceries
at the check-out counter. Inflation is not a factor;
as prices rise, packages shrink.
Penny Russell, artist, Sewickley, Pennsylvania

815. WRITING A SCREENPLAY   One page of an
average screenplay equals about one minute of screen
time. Therefore, the script for a typical feature film
should be about a hundred pages long. In fact, many
studios and producers won't look at screenplays much
longer than a hundred pages.
John Griesemer, writer and actor, New York City

816. USING PULLEYS   Two pulleys connected by a
belt should be separated by at least the difference
between their individual diameters.
John H. Parker, mechanical engineer

817. JOGGING   If you can run one and a half miles
in twelve minutes, six days a week, you can run any
distance you like.   *Dr. Larry R. Hunt, Toronto, Ontario*

818. CABINETMAKING   Sanding is 10 percent of any cabinetmaking job.   *Joel Warren, cabinetmaker*

819. BUYING EQUIPMENT   Don't buy a new piece of equipment for your business unless it can pay for itself in three months.   *Kevin Kelly, Athens, Georgia*

820. MAKING A MOVIE   Some types of scenes are harder to shoot than others. For dialogue scenes, you will need to shoot about 4 feet of film for every foot you use. For scenes without dialogue, the ratio is more like two or three to one.
Christopher Wordsworth, film maker

821. RUNNING A CLUB   Don't expect more than one third of any professional-club members to attend a meeting. Build up a large membership so there are enough members around to make up for those who are away or otherwise engaged.
Dr. Barbara Pletcher, National Association of Professional Saleswomen, Sacramento, California

822. EXHALING   A healthy adult should be able to completely exhale a deep breath in three seconds.
James Macmillan, M.D.

823. CHECKING THE TEMPERATURE   One way to check the temperature when you're outdoors is to inhale rapidly. If you feel the moisture in your nostrils begin to freeze, it is 10 degrees Fahrenheit or colder.
Truman Plant, expressman

824. BUYING A CAR   By the time you finish paying for them, most cars will be worth about $1000 and will constantly need minor repairs. So anyone who can do minor repairs on a car should only spend $1000 to buy one in the first place.
Bill Marsh, printer

825. BUYING GROCERIES   Groceries cost about $10 to $12 per bag.   *Rick Eckstrom, builder*

826. DIETING   Most overeating happens at night. If you can't diet all the time, diet after dark.
Arthur Phillips, Fort Myers, Florida

827. SMOKING CIGARETTES Take twenty-five milligrams of vitamin C for every cigarette you smoke.
Bob Horton, statistics consultant, West Lafayette, Indiana

828. COOKING BEANS Eight quarts of dried beans will feed one hundred people.
The Lansing Methodist Church Women's Society

829. EATING FRIJOLES A rule of thumb (that I just learned today): Don't eat frijoles and tortillas for supper the night before a long meeting.
Barbara F. Baun, librarian, Benson, Arizona

830. DEALING WITH DOUBT (GOING TO WORK) Sometimes you can't tell if you feel good enough to go to work. When in doubt, go.
Gael W. Hoyt, San Bernardino, California

831. USING A CHAIN SAW A logger can control the path of a falling tree by notching the trunk in the direction of fall. For safety's sake, a notch or front cut should be used to fell any tree over 6 inches in diameter. *Ned Bounds, sawyer, Salmon, Idaho*

832. USING CONCRETE BLOCKS Concrete block walls can be laid without mortar and finished with surface bonding cement. Never assemble more than three courses of dry block without checking the wall for plumb. *Albert Snyder, Albuquerque, New Mexico*

833. MAKING BOOKS About one fifth of the cost of producing a book is in the cost of its paper.
Marshall Lee, bookmaker

834. BUYING PAPER FOR A BOOK You can determine the amount of paper you will need to produce a book by taking a book about the same size and kind as yours will be and weighing it. If it weighs one pound and you are making 5000 books, you know you should order 5000 pounds of paper. The cover of the book you weigh will account for spoilage and then some. *Marshall Lee, bookmaker*

835. MELTING METAL A pound of coke will melt twenty pounds of bronze or nine pounds of iron.
C. W. Ammens, founder

836. HITCHHIKING When you're hitchhiking, look like who you want to pick you up.
Stewart Brand, publisher, The CoEvolution Quarterly

837. LEAVING A SUBMARINE If you find yourself in a submarine, add the number of times you have descended to the number of times you have surfaced, and divide the total by two. If there is one left over, don't open the hatch.
Lori Janulis, Ithaca, New York, quoting an old Reader's Digest

838. SHIMMING A CRACK When you are restoring furniture, it is a good idea to shim, rather than fill, any cracks more than 1/32 inch wide. It takes a little more time but you should be able to make and set a shim in about half an hour.
Tom "Tex" Tolson, The Family Handyman magazine

839. WORKING IN YOSEMITE NATIONAL PARK
Working one year as a park ranger in Yosemite is
equal to working twelve years in any other national
park.   *Scott M. Kruse, Yosemite National Park, California*

840. DRINKING VODKA   You need four cans of tomato juice for one bottle of vodka. You need four bottles of vodka and one package of lemons per bottle of
hot sauce.   *David A. Lloyd-Jones, Tokyo, Japan*

841. DESIGNING A GUN   A safe rule, if you want
to design a gun with recoil that is not too unpleasant,
is to make the gun weigh at least ninety-six times the
load of shot it is built to fire.
W. W. Greener, arms maker, from The Gun and Its Development
(written in the 1800s)

842. ARRANGING FLOWERS   Some color schemes
are less risky than others. Three strong colors to a
quiet one is usually a pleasing proportion.
Christine Newberry, retired teacher

843. CHOOSING A HORSE   To avoid looking silly
on a horse, choose a mount whose withers are the
height of your shoulders.   *Michael Rider, art director*

844. PLAYING VIDEO GAMES   To avoid looking
like a beginner, plan on spending $5 the first time you
play a video game. If you don't have $5, watch some-
one else play $5 worth.   *Trevor Poole, video game hotshot*

845. RECOGNIZING A BUREAUCRAT   You can
be fairly sure you are dealing with a bureaucrat if he
or she has to dial 9 to get an outside line.
Burnham Kelly, Ithaca, New York

846. FLYING A KITE   A wind that rustles leaves
and that you can barely feel on your face is blowing
from four to seven miles an hour. A wind moving
about twelve miles an hour will keep tree leaves in
constant motion. This is the upper limit for most kite
flying. If the wind if lifting loose paper off the ground
and raising dust, it is too strong for the average kite.
Tal Streeter, kite builder

847. PAINTING A HOUSE It takes the average person one hour to paint 1000 square feet, plus one hour for each window or door.
Rebecca Crowell, artist, Tempe, Arizona

848. FIXING A LEEK It takes fifteen seconds for the average geek to harvest and wash off the average leek. *James Macmillan, M.D.*

849. PRICING YOUR WORK To price a quilt, sweater, or similar piece of handiwork, multiply the cost of your materials by three. The resulting figure should represent a reasonable hourly wage while keeping the price in what most people consider the affordable bracket. *Carol Terrizzi, graphic designer*

850. EARNING MONEY After thirty, a highly qualified professional can expect to earn his or her age, times $1000, in salary.
Karen E. O'Neill, career consultant, Englewood, Colorado

851. ORDERING FRENCH FRIES The counter help in fast-food restaurants will usually try to sell you some French fries if you don't include any in your order. As a rule, one out of five customers will accept their offer. The score for hot cherry pies is somewhat lower.
Nancy, McDonald's restaurant counter help

852. PANNING FOR GOLD A good miner, doing a careful job of panning, can handle about six pans per hour, or sixty in ten hours — about one third of a cubic yard of gravel. An expert working in sandy gravel without much clay or hardpan might double this, panning two thirds of a cubic yard in a day. Under the most favorable conditions, a yard a day is just about the top limit for panning.
William F. Boericke, gold miner

853. THE CHRISTMAS TREE RULE OF THREE
To find out how many lights your Christmas tree needs, multiply the tree height times the tree width times three.
Michael Spencer, lawyer, San Francisco, California

854. THE TRASH RULE OF THREE You have to look through a wastebasket three times to find a missing piece of paper. *Anne Herbert, writer*

855. THE PEEPER RULE OF THREE Don't count on spring until you've heard the peepers in full voice for three consecutive nights.
James McConkey, writer, Trumansburg, New York

856. GROWING CORN Your corn should be knee-high by the Fourth of July.
Nancy Dunn, production manager, Sausalito, California, and countless other people

857. DIGGING A POST HOLE A hole for a cattle-fence post should be an arm's length deep, plus the length of your fingers.
Adrienne Garreau, farmer

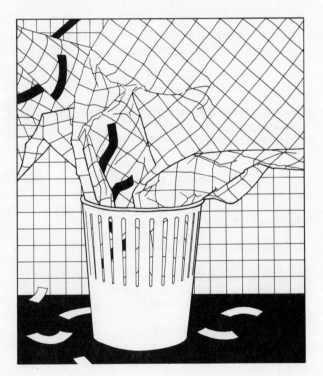

858. SAGGING HOUSES There is cause for concern if the ridge of a house sags more than 1/2 inch per year. *Albert Snyder, Albuquerque, New Mexico*

859. STALKING DEER When you are stalking deer (or "still-hunting" as the experts call it), patience and an extremely slow pace are essential. If you travel more than a quarter of a mile in an hour, you are traveling too fast. *J. P. Thomas, still-hunter*

860. SEATING YOUR GUESTS To be sure that each diner has plenty of table room, space your guests on 30-inch centers.
The Joy of Cooking

861. TRANSPORTING FISH Iced fish keeps better than fish refrigerated at 32 degrees Fahrenheit. You will need about one pound of crushed ice for every two pounds of fish.
Kenn and Pat Oberrecht, commercial fishers

862. HELPING A CUSTOMER LOAD LUMBER If there is an odd number of items, let the customer load the first one. If there is an even number of items, let the customer load the first two.
Anonymous lumber yard worker

863. RULE OF OUTDOOR CONSTRUCTION When raindrops hit your windshield faster than you can count them, it's time to knock off work for the day. *Gene Beitel, contractor*

864. HIRING CONSTRUCTION WORKERS Two workers can do three times as much work as one. Three workers can do four times as much work as one. Four workers can do four times as much work as one.
Rick Lazarus, residential contractor, Spencer, New York

865. HIRING BOYS One boy's a boy; two boys — half a boy; three boys — no boy at all.
Margaret "Granny" Cochron, 102 years old

866. THROWING A FRISBEE A Frisbee will crack and break when you can see your breath.
Grady Wells, editor

867. CHOKING ON FOOD   If a choking person can verbally request the Heimlich maneuver, he or she doesn't need it.   *James Macmillan, M.D.*

868. CHURCH HEALTH   The amount of participation required of the congregation is a good indicator of a church's health. If you have fifty-five jobs per one hundred members, you have a growing church. If you have twenty-six jobs your church is holding even. Fewer jobs indicate a church in decline.
Steve Parker, aerospace engineer, Princeton, New Jersey

869. PACKING A PISTOL   The handle of your holstered revolver should hang midway between your wrist and your elbow with your arms at your side.
Alan Ladd, in the movie Shane, *1953*

870. LOOKING THROUGH YOUR POCKETS   It takes almost twice as long to find something in your coat pockets when you are not wearing your coat. If you have a flight jacket or parka with more than four pockets, you can usually save time by putting it on just to look through the pockets.
Gerald Gutlipp, mathematician

871. SPOTTING A SPY   One out of every three Soviet or Soviet-bloc diplomats in this country is a spy or has some sort of intelligence-gathering responsibility.   *William Webster, FBI Director*

872. MAKING A SNOWSHOE   You can tailor-make a snowshoe by having the intended user hold his or her arms in a circle, just touching at the fingertips. The size of the loop formed by the arms is the size of the snowshoe frame.
Anonymous American Indian snowshoe-maker

873. STORING SEEDS AT ROOM TEMPERATURE   If you are storing seeds at room temperature, each percentage point you reduce their moisture content will approximately double their longevity.
J. L. Hudson, seedsman, Redwood City, California

874. CAPTURING GIANT SNAKES   For capturing pythons, anacondas, boas and other large constrictors, it is wise to have one person for every 4 or 5 feet of snake.   *Donald R. Gentner, Cardiff by the Sea, California*

875. GROWING MARIJUANA   One skilled California marijuana grower can properly maintain thirty-three plants. Two growers can maintain one hundred plants.

J. K., Harvest Moon Growers, Mendocino and Humboldt, California

876. TELLING DAY FROM NIGHT   During Ramadan, the sacred ninth month of the Moslem year, fasting is practiced daily from sunrise to sunset. For people lacking better indicators, the point when day becomes night is the point when you can't tell a black thread from a white one.

George Sheldon, artist and traveler

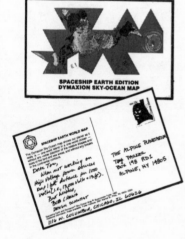

**SPACESHIP EARTH EDITION
DYMAXION SKY-OCEAN MAP**

877. STORING SEEDS AT LOW TEMPERATURE   If you are keeping seeds in cold storage, each 10 degrees Fahrenheit you lower their temperature will double their longevity.

J. L. Hudson, seedsman, Redwood City, California

878. LOOKING FOR EXTRATERRESTRIAL DUST   Hoping to find samples of cosmic dust, NASA scientists carefully inspect tiny particles captured by high-flying planes. They have a rule of thumb: If a particle is large enough to see without a microscope, it is probably contamination of their sample and not extraterrestrial debris.

Dr. Uel Clanton, associate curator for cosmic dust, Johnson Space Center

879. WRITING SOMETHING IMPORTANT   If you feel that you need a thesaurus to write something, you are probably trying too hard.

John Shed, language instructor

880. CAUSING A SPARK   Electricity will arc, or jump a gap of, about 1/4 inch for each ten thousand volts. This rule is often used by TV repairmen and electronic technicians to quickly check a high-voltage power supply, a practice that is not recommended for the novice.

Renard Braun, physicist

881. BUYING A GOOD PAIR OF MEN'S PANTS
The measurement from the crotch to the waistband
on a pair of pants is called the rise. A man who is
shorter than 5 feet 6 inches should buy pants with a
short rise. A man who is between 5 feet 6 and 5 feet
9 needs a regular rise. Anyone taller than that should
have a long rise. *B. W., quoting from Esquire magazine*

882. CHANGING YOUR OIL   If your car holds five
quarts of engine oil or more, change the oil every
three thousand miles. For every half quart less than
five that your engine holds, decrease your between-
change mileage by five hundred. For example, a car
that has an oil capacity of three and a half quarts
should have its oil changed every fifteen hundred
miles. *Will Parker, Georgian music authority*

883. ORGANIZING PEOPLE   The people who stay
at a demonstration when it starts to rain are the ones
you can count on.
*Anonymous, dedicated to a University of California at Davis draft
demonstration*

884. WATCHING YOUR CHICKENS   If your
chickens run for cover when it starts to rain, the
shower will be brief. If they stay outside, it is going
to rain all day.
Lewis and Paulette Ramsey, Howardsville, Virginia

885. CARING FOR A HORSE   You should allow at
least one hour per day to feed and groom a horse.
Mary Flinn, Starlane Farms, Lansing, New York

886. DESIGNING A SUBMARINE   A submarine
will move through the water most efficiently if it has
a length-to-beam ratio of between 10 to 1 and 13 to 1.
Brent Wiggans, artist and military buff

887. DRUNKEN DIVERS   The deeper a scuba
diver descends the more nitrogen he absorbs from the
air he is breathing. Increased levels of nitrogen in the
blood cause an intoxicating condition known as nitrogen narcosis or "rapture of the deep." Divers will
often use martinis as a rough measure of narcosis:
each 50 feet of depth makes you feel as disoriented as
one martini on an empty stomach.
W. Suter, Arlington, Virginia

888. PREDICTING RAIN The heaviest rainfall usually comes three to five days after the new and full moons. *Robert B. Thomas, The Old Farmer's Almanac*

889. CELLARING WINE When cellaring a wine, add about one year of aging time for every two degrees the cellar averages below 65 degrees Fahrenheit.
Craig Goldwyn, president, The Beverage Testing Institute

890. BUYING WINE As a rule, the returns from a bottle of wine diminish as the price increases. A $10 wine is usually better than a $5 wine, but never twice as good.
Craig Goldwyn, president, The Beverage Testing Institute

891. FITTING A MAN'S JACKET You can check the length of a dress jacket with your arms relaxed at your sides. The hem of the jacket should reach the tip of your thumbs. *Danny Speer, composer*

892. REGARDING ROMANCE If you need to talk about it, you probably shouldn't do it.
Robbie Aceto, musician

893. FINDING A HOMETOWN You can still consider an area your hometown if you know your old friends' phone numbers by heart.
Martha Farnsworth Riche, editor

894. COMMUTING IN TOKYO In Tokyo a bicycle is faster than a car for most trips of less than 50 minutes. The same is true against trains, except during rush hours; then the break point is about 30 minutes. A motorcycle, ridden carefully but without regard for the law, is twice as fast as a car.
David Lloyd-Jones, Tokyo, Japan.

895. BUTTERING BREAD One pound of butter will spread three to four pounds of sandwich bread.
The Joy of Cooking

896. DEALING WITH DOUBT When in doubt, don't.
R. Buckminster Fuller, architect and inventor of the geodesic dome

INDEX

This is really two indexes in one. The more than five hundred specific entries will help you find a particular rule of thumb. There are also general entries (in capital letters) that comprise large, more whimsical groups of rules that resemble each other for one reason or another.